The World of Failing Machines

Speculative Realism and Literature

The World of Failing Machines

Speculative Realism and Literature

Grant Hamilton

Winchester, UK
Washington, USA

First published by Zero Books, 2016
Zero Books is an imprint of John Hunt Publishing Ltd., Laurel House, Station Approach,
Alresford, Hants, SO24 9JH, UK
office1@jhpbooks.net
www.johnhuntpublishing.com
www.zero-books.net

For distributor details and how to order please visit the 'Ordering' section on our website.

Text copyright: Grant Hamilton 2015

ISBN: 978 1 78535 324 6
Library of Congress Control Number: 2016931752

A CIP catalogue record for this book is available from the British Library.

Design: Lee Nash

Printed and bound by CPI Group (UK) Ltd, Croydon, CR0 4YY, UK

We operate a distinctive and ethical publishing philosophy in all areas of our business, from our global network of authors to production and worldwide distribution.

CONTENTS

For M.H.[4]

Introduction
Speculative Realism and Correlationism

This book arises from a very simple question – what would a speculative-realist literary criticism look like? I had stumbled across speculative realism in a rather curious way. I had been reading into the ecological crisis and the relationship it had with a rapacious capitalism. George Monbiot's *Feral* (2014) led me to Naomi Klein's *This Changes Everything* (2014), which in turn encouraged me to revisit the work of Cheryll Glotfelty in an attempt to bring these environmental and political issues back to my own area of research – literary studies. While talking through this material with a colleague over lunch, he suddenly asked whether my reading had also included Timothy Morton's *Hyperobjects* (2013). I admitted it had not. Without looking, he delved into his bag to retrieve a copy of Morton's book. "Read this," he said, pushing the book towards me across the lunch table. "It shifts ecocriticism into genuinely new territories." He picked up his fork and continued eating. It took less than a day to read Morton's book, and by the time I had finished it I had been overwhelmed by a dramatically new way of thinking about the world – a way of thinking that has emerged from what is today known as speculative realism.

After reading Morton's book, I endeavored to read backwards (as it were) into the key texts of speculative realism so that I could understand better the philosophical moorings of *Hyperobjects*. Since nearly every book on the subject began with a reprise of the movement's genesis, I learned rather quickly that speculative realism had come into being some seven years before my encounter with Morton's book. On Friday 27 April, 2007, Goldsmiths College in London held a one-day workshop dedicated to showcasing and discussing the merits of what was described in the abstract of the event as "a variety of research programs committed to upholding the autonomy of reality." The workshop was titled "Speculative Realism," and in this moment a new movement was born.

Or, it would have been if not for what one of the speakers called "a ferocious disagreement" amongst the participants (Harman 2011b, 171). Although those gathered maintained some kind of belief in a material reality that existed in its own right beyond the human mind, none could agree about either the significance of such an observation or *how* one might even talk of such a world. For some of the participants, the human was not and could never be in a position to know the world as it is. The human/world relationship, they argued, was always mediated through something – be that through language, thought, perception, or something else. Other participants championed the idea that the world did indeed give itself up to the enquiring mind under certain circumstances, one example being the rule of mathematics. Even those who initially seemed to agree with each other eventually discovered over the course of the day that they had radically different readings of the same philosophical works that took their ideas in fundamentally different directions. As such, those who led the workshop – Iain Hamilton Grant, Ray Brassier, Quentin Meillassoux, and Graham Harman – demonstrated perfectly well that a shared commitment to the "autonomy of reality" was not enough to sustain an entire philosophical movement. At its very inception, speculative realism had seemingly exploded into a vast number of splinter cells that ultimately bore little similarity to one another.

But still there was a kernel of something, a shared interest in addition to the defense of some version of realism, which brought together the work of these warring factions. And that kernel was *correlationism*. Correlationism arrived via the pen of Quentin Meillassoux as a means of describing what he thought of as the single most important idea of contemporary continental philosophy – the idea that we literally cannot think of the world

2

as independent from the human mind that perceives it. For Meillassoux, this correlation between mind and world had dominated continental philosophy to such an extent that the task of nigh-on every philosopher since Descartes had simply been to map in one way or another the essential relationship between thought and being. However, the expense of doing so was profound. As Meillassoux makes clear in his introduction of the term here, *correlationism loses a whole world of things*:

> Correlationism takes many forms, but particularly those of transcendental philosophy, the varieties of phenomenology, and post-modernism. But although these currents are all extraordinarily varied in themselves, they all share, according to me, a more or less explicit decision: that there are no objects, no events, no laws, no beings which are not always-already correlated with a point of view, with a subjective access. (qtd. in Gratton 2014, 14)

In other words, correlationism describes a way of thinking about a world of things that exists only to the extent to which it exists "for us." So, a tree, the world, the universe exists only when it becomes thinkable – which is the same as saying that everything we have yet to discover (for example an alien life-form on another planet) does not (yet) exist. Put another way, "correlationism consists in disqualifying the claim that it is possible to consider the realms of subjectivity and objectivity independently of one another" (Meillassoux 2009, 5). Importantly, it is when this disqualification is put in place that the world of things "out there" is irretrievably lost to us, "the thinking subject." If one accepts the disqualification then the only questions that philosophy is left to contemplate are not those concerned with reality-in-itself but rather those about "how we come to know the world, or the ideas we form about it, or the relationships among these ideas, or the cultural and linguistic features that block us from reality as it is" (Gratton 2014, 5). And for Meillassoux, this is exactly what contemporary continental philosophy has become – a philosophy of the subject, for it accepted many years ago the disqualification that put an end to the objectivity of objects.

That being said, one should not mistake correlationism for an unwieldy blunt hammer brought to bear on thinking about the world. As Meillassoux makes clear, as a style of thought correlationism presents in a number of different ways – from a subtle instantiation, which Meillassoux regards as a "weak" form of correlationism, to a rather less refined, and for that more obvious, "strong" variety.

From the beginning, the weakest strain of correlationism concedes that an external reality not only exists but that we can also think it. However, it does so only to then deny the claim that because we can think or theorize a mind-independent reality we can therefore go on to *know* the world around us. According to correlationist thought, we cannot. The world as it is – its essential nature or character – is inaccessible to us. And it is so *precisely because we are human!* This startling claim is one inherited from Immanuel Kant, the eighteenth-century German philosopher who carved the world into the *noumenal* (the world "as it is") and the *phenomenal* (the world "as it appears to be") and in so doing forever barred the human from making direct contact with the objects of the world. One of the most striking observations in Kant's *Critique of Pure Reason* (1781) – a text that most practicing philosophers in the West consider to be *the* foundational text of contemporary philosophy – is that this kind of knowledge of the world is only and always a function of the way in which the human mind structures its experience. For this reason, Kant concluded that the best examination of the world is one that recognizes this fact and therefore interrogates the world through the way in which it presents itself to us. In other words, the fact that we are humans interrogating the world means that we are best served by considering the realm of the phenomenal – of

4

impressions and experience. Outside of this, Kant maintains, the human can know nothing with authority.

If this seems like a radical conclusion to draw, know that it is a conclusion that Kant tempers from the far more radical account of perception given by the earlier Anglo-Irish philosopher George Berkeley. Indeed, it is Berkeley who perhaps best represents the species of "strong correlationism" that Meillassoux discusses. Of course, Berkeley is noted today for his ideas on subjective idealism, which is the belief that reality is completely dependent upon the minds of those who perceive it. For Berkeley, a world of mind-independent objects is a fallacy that the mind creates for itself. If the world could be said to exist at all then it could only do so as a product of a mind that perceives it. Perhaps the phrase that captures most accurately the character of Berkeley's bold sense of things is one that Berkeley himself offered in his *Treatise Concerning the Principles of Human Knowledge* (1710) – the beautiful English/Latin hybrid assertion of *esse is percipi,* which simply means, "to be is to be perceived."

Yet, regardless of whether one talks in terms of a weak or strong correlationism, the point that Meillassoux wishes us to take away here is that correlationist thought in its various guises has dominated the discipline of what we might think of as contemporary philosophy. It has done so by demanding that the philosopher not only take notice of the mind regarding itself in relation to questions concerning metaphysics but that the philosopher also places that same self-regarding mind at the very center of *every* consideration of the world. Nothing evidences the point more directly than René Descartes's infamous dictum, "I think therefore I am" (1637). Commonly known to even the non-philosopher, Descartes's assertion emerges solely from a mind regarding itself and as such can be parsed in this simple way: "I am here because of my mind" (actually because of my ability to doubt my existence) and, by extension, "the world is here because I can think it." Kant's account of reality is, I think it is fair to say, more rich and nuanced than Descartes's, and Berkeley's more aggressively driven by the Ideal. But even so, these giants of philosophy – Kant, Berkeley, and Descartes – all ultimately describe a world that is only understandable through the mediation, in one way or another, of the human mind.

It is then this observation that the four speakers at Goldsmiths College took issue with in their own philosophies.[1] Iain Hamilton Grant saw the proper response to correlationism necessitate a return to the work of the nineteenth-century German philosopher Friedrich Schelling in order to think again about "Nature." In a heady mix of *prius* (Schelling's absolute prior to substances), non-vitalism, and Idealism, which leads to the observation that nature is a "demonstration of the constancy of production, of power *always at work*, always *intrinsic* to the formative process" (Grant 2011, 45), Grant speculates on the character of the unknowable productivity of nature in an attempt to understand from where both subjects and objects arise.

Ray Brassier, on the other hand, responded to correlationism by swimming entirely different philosophical waters. For Brassier, correlationism raises fundamental questions about the constitution of the "I" that surveys the world. Indeed, in his book *Nihil Unbound* (2007), Brassier reveals it to be, along with a philosophy that he sees as in thrall to the various characters of the subject, nothing more than the "pathetic twinge of human self-esteem" (2007, xi). It is a robust assertion that ultimately takes his philosophy down a line of thought that leads towards a nihilism that he sees as:

the unavoidable corollary of the realist conviction that there is a mind-independent reality, which, despite the presumptions of human narcissism, is indifferent to our existence and oblivious to the "values" and "meanings" which we would drape over it in order to make it more hospitable. (2007, xi)

Meillassoux makes a similar observation about the significance of the surveying subject but refuses to follow Brassier into a discussion of nihilism. "The world can do without humanity" (2009, 136), Meillassoux asserts, but not because of an inescapable Brasserian trajectory towards "The End." Rather, the world can do without us because it has already done without humanity for such a long time. Indeed, for Meillassoux science has shown without question that time (and space) existed long before any of us were cognizant of it, and that means that we must acknowledge the "Great Outdoors" as something that is not simply a correlate of human thought. The world we experience, Meillassoux claims, is a material reality that prefigures not only Kant's categories of thought but every form of correlationism. For sure, it is a material reality that looks very strange to us – it is what Meillassoux describes as the condition of possibility for every subject and object of the world, and that means it is also the space of radical contingency or uncertainty – but it is a material reality, Meillassoux argues, that we *can* get to know. Through mathematics, our world presents itself as a plenum of pure chaos, a world in which what is ultimately real is the "hyper-chaos" of a never-ending game of probability.

But if what is ultimately real is pure chaos, then what of all the non-chaotic discrete forms that we see in the world? Such is the question posed by the American philosopher Graham Harman. For Harman, Meillassoux's discussion of chaos avoids the very *things* that we encounter in the world on a daily basis. So, he sets about writing an object-oriented philosophy – which is to say, a philosophy that recognizes and respects the objects of the world as things-in-themselves. Like Kant, Harman writes that although we can regard a mind-independent world of objects, we can never fully know this world. Objects remain forever beyond our grasp not because of a failure in our ability to engineer a satisfactory way to interrogate the world, but rather because the relationship itself that emerges between us and a world of objects simply cannot fully translate an object under enquiry. That is to say, we can pick up a stone, turn it over in our hands, consider its texture, smell it, taste it even, but as far as Harman is concerned these moments of interrogation will never reveal the essential quality of the stone. The stone will always be this set of sense impressions and (much) more.

And it is with this observation that one can begin to understand the significant way in which Harman's view of the world departs from that of Kant. While our inability to access the essential quality of the stone (that is, the noumenal aspect of the stone) makes Kant put the human first in every consideration of the world, for Harman *such inaccessibility is experienced by every object in every encounter that it has with every other object*. That is to say, just like the human who cannot fully apprehend the essence of the stone by experiencing it, neither can the rain as it falls upon the stone, the fly which rests upon it, nor the ground upon which it sits. None of these encounters *exhausts* the essence of the stone. And for this reason, Harman thinks of the human relationship with the world as functionally unremarkable. In other words, unlike Kant, Harman refuses the idea that the human/world relation is privileged over any other relation between objects. His conclusion is that the human/stone relation is of exactly the same order as the rain/stone relation, the fly/stone relation, the ground/stone relation, and so on and so forth.

It is then the sheer diversity of directions presented in the work of these writers (and others) who have reacted to the reign of correlationism in contemporary continental philosophy that means we should take seriously Harman's passing comment that "all it takes to be a speculative realist is to be opposed to correlationism" (2013, 5). Indeed, it seems clear that membership of this group cannot be based on anything more substantial than this rather casual observation. While this surely means that the term itself is a little too broad to be useful within the domain of philosophy proper, nonetheless I think it invokes enough intellectual curiosity and intrigue to still be useful to the non-philosopher. That is to say, my sense is that the way in which speculative realism highlights an on-going concern with a mind-independent reality and the imposition of correlationism as a critical horizon to be conscious of and perhaps to transgress, means that speculative realism *as an idea or concept* carries enough weight to make it valuable to disciplines outside of philosophy. To me, it is no surprise that as I sit down to write this book, speculative realism has already made itself felt in such diverse fields of study as the fine arts, architecture, and medieval studies. My wager is that it will have a similar impact in the field of literary studies, given time. As such, Timothy Morton's *Hyperobjects*, a book that has already injected some new thought and vocabulary into the field of ecocriticism, can be seen as metonymic of a wider revisionary agenda. In literary studies, it may herald the beginning of a genuinely new way of thinking about and reading literature, one that is enlivened by a confrontation with correlationism.

This book then is an attempt to plot the coordinates by which speculative realism might make itself felt in the study of literature. But, as our previous observation on the diversity of writing brought together under the mantle of speculative realism might suggest, we cannot begin until we have announced which species of speculative realism has our full attention. For me, the object-oriented approach of writers such as Graham Harman, Timothy Morton, and Levi Bryant raises interesting questions for the study of literature in a way that the other variants of speculative realism do not – what, for example, should the literary critic do with Brassier's strain of nihilism? It is therefore Harman's breed of speculative realism that I will follow in this book. As such, the reader should be aware that when I write of "speculative realism" here, unless otherwise stated, I am referring to a narrowed sense of the term that speaks only to object-oriented philosophy.

Because of this conscious turn to Graham Harman's work, I think it is fair to say that on the whole we will be taking something of a Kantian view of things here – that is, the world for us is divided between an unknowable essential reality (the noumenal) and an aesthetic realm which is the only reality to which we have access (the phenomenal). However, with that being said, we will take our lead from those moments of divergence from such Kantian thought that have come to characterize object-oriented philosophy. We do so because such moments of divergence, at least as I see it, inaugurate a radical challenge to both the architecture and act of literary criticism. Put simply, if one is to take seriously the claims of speculative realism then not only the way in which we think about literature but also the way in which we write about literature must be radically altered. In other words, if the literary critic is to remain faithful to the basic tenets of speculative realism then we must "do" literature in a fundamentally different way to that practiced in English departments up and down the land. This book offers a glimpse of what such a radically revised literary criticism might look like.

To this end, we begin in chapter one by considering the place of meaning in a world where things exist outside of and independent to the human mind. The question of meaning and where it is to be found in relation to the literary text has been something that has occupied the minds of literary scholars for generations. Speculative realism offers us yet another way to conceptualize the locale of meaning in literature, and in so doing it encourages us to reconsider the significance of the act of speculation. What is speculation, we must ask, and what is it that speculative realism speculates on?

The second chapter begins our conversation between philosophy and literature in an explicit way. The world of objects invigorated through speculative realism seems to lead us towards a particular kind of literature – that of French Symbolism. At first glance, writers such as Baudelaire and

Mallarmé seemed to imagine the world in very similar terms to those outlined by today's object-oriented philosophers. But is this literature as good a fit with speculative realism as it first appears?

Chapter three transitions from the study of literature proper to a discussion of literary theory. Our concern here is explaining why a literary criticism that is informed by object-oriented philosophy cannot be the same kind of criticism as that written by those in the twentieth-century. Even though thinking of the literary text as an object in its own right might suggest certain alliances with previous styles of criticism, it is clear that something new is required in order to remain faithful to the basic tenets of speculative realism.

In extending the critique of the previous chapter, chapter four goes on to posit the literary text as a failing machine. Here the main influences are from the recent work of Levi Bryant, who charts a machine-oriented ontology, the writings of the hugely important French philosopher Gilles Deleuze, and an idea of "literariness" that emerged from the work of a group of literary and cultural critics who practiced their art in the early decades of the twentieth century.

Chapter five responds to the fact that a reconsideration of the literary text as a (failing) machine demands a similar reconsideration of the reader as machine. And with this observation, a machine-oriented ontology emerges that makes clear that what arises from the encounter between the machinic reader and the literary text/machine is a new machine, a new machinic assemblage that we should call the reading machine. It is the character and capacity of this reading machine that this chapter explores.

The sixth chapter reflects on the discussions that we have held in the previous chapters and in so doing introduces some of the first steps that others have made in defining the shape of this new literary criticism informed by the concerns of speculative realism. However, it is by critiquing these first steps that this chapter looks to chart its own program by which the literary critic can conduct a criticism that is sympathetic to the tenets of an object-oriented philosophy. That is to say, it is here that I outline what I think a speculative-realist literary criticism might look like.

The last chapter offers some closing thoughts on the relationship between speculative realism and literature.

The test of any new literary theory or style of criticism is what it empowers critics to see or do that has not already been seen or done. The question for us, then, is what kind of motivation is put in place or what new spaces of enquiry and critique are opened up by a literary criticism that is faithful to the concerns of speculative realism? We begin our exploration of this question by thinking about meaning in the literary text and the act of speculation.

1

Speculating on a World of Meaning

What does it profit a philosopher if he gains knowledge but loses the whole world? In the course of the last two centuries of philosophy [...] we have indeed lost the world, and it is a world most badly lost. (Braver 2013, 11)

As far as the philosopher is concerned, we start our exploration of the implications of speculative realism on the study of literature from a rather controversial position. We start from the idea that the world around us is real; that it is not an effect of human perception or cognition but that it exists independently of our ability to comprehend it. It is a controversial position not only because it goes against nearly everything that has been written in continental philosophy over the last two centuries, but because it is a position that most informed writers claim inevitably leads back to a regressive, naive account of the Real.

But how naive is this sense of the Real? The answer to such a question seems to rest on the kind of claims that one is willing to make about the world – can I know the world? Do I have unrestricted access to the essential being of everyday objects? Given enough time, can I know what everything *is*? For the contemporary philosopher, naivety seems to present itself at the very moment that the human is figured outside of an account of the world. Why? Because the world, it is argued, can only be understood as "our world." To think otherwise is, as the Slovenian philosopher Slavoj Žižek writes, pure fantasy.

This is the fundamental subjective position of fantasy: to be reduced to a gaze observing the world in the condition of the subject's non-existence [...] "The world without us" is thus fantasy at its purest: witnessing the Earth itself regaining its precastrated sense of innocence. (qtd. in Gratton 2014, 52)

Here, Žižek paints a picture of fantasy – which he reads as the manifestation of a desire to escape from the harsh reality of the world – emerging as a symptom of a naive belief that our senses report an unmediated or untranslated vision of the world *as it is*. But this is not at all what the object-oriented species of speculative realism posits. Graham Harman's position is that there is indeed a world of objects that is independent to the function of the human mind, but that we cannot gain direct access to it – that our speculations about Kant's noumenal plane of reality must remain precisely that, speculation.

This, though, has radical consequences for how we can claim to navigate the world in which we live. If we are forever barred from accessing the world "as it is" (rather than "as it appears to be"), then how can one account for our success in knowing and representing it? "Surely," the anti-realist philosopher would say, "a truly mind-independent world would make any representation of it, in thought or language, unreliable, if not impossible. On what grounds can we trust our theories if they could all be radically mistaken?" (Khlentzos, 2001).[2]

The riposte of the speculative realist is twofold. First is the assertion that we can trust our theories about the world only to the extent that we realize that they grant an imperfect account of things. For the speculative realist, any knowledge of the world that can be put into service is discursive in character and that means it is ultimately unreliable. Here, discourse equals unreliability because discourse is always the product of an act of translation that necessarily distorts, modifies, or in some way changes the initial object of enquiry. The literary scholar as well as the scientist has been comfortable with this world of transient truths and uncertainty since at least the beginning of the twentieth century, but we can perhaps turn to the literary translator as best evidence for the claim that the act of translation deforms its object of interest.

Translation is immediately thought of as a game of substitution – one language code for another. However, if we spend any time at all thinking about the act of translation, it quickly becomes clear that it is much more complicated than this. Susan Bassnett, who is perhaps the foremost authority on the subject of translation, begins her book *Translation Studies* (1980) by saying that the act of translation has always been perceived as "a 'mechanical' rather than a 'creative' process" (1994, 2). But, as she goes on to explain, this view of things is entirely wrong. For Bassnett, it is certain that one can never again mistake translation for a mechanical industry once one understands that the translator is not only engaged with the individual words on the page but also the implicit sense that emerges from the various contexts in which those words appear. Put simply, it is the tension that arises between words and meaning that makes the task of the translator a difficult one. The translator must constantly negotiate between linguistic fidelity on the one hand and the meaning of linguistic forms in particular cultural contexts on the other. As usual, the Italian semiotician, philosopher, and best-selling fiction writer Umberto Eco makes things clear with an excellent example of the translator's dilemma:

Let us suppose that in a novel a character says, *You're just pulling my leg*. To render such an idiom in Italian by *stai solo tirandomi la gamba* or *tu stai menandomi per la gamba* would be literally correct but misleading. In Italian one should say *mi stai prendendo per il naso*, thus substituting an English leg with an Italian nose. If literally translated, the English expression, absolutely unusual in Italian, would make the reader suppose that the character [...] was inventing a provocative rhetorical figure – which is completely misleading as in English the expression is a simple idiom. By choosing *nose* instead of *leg* a translator puts the Italian reader in the same situation as the English one. Thus only by being *literally unfaithful* can a translator succeed in being truly faithful to the source text. (2003, 5)

As we will see in chapter four, exploring conclusions such as this – that the most faithful translation can be the result of the most unfaithful translation of the original text – is the bread and butter of literature and literary criticism. But our point to take away here is that in order to transmit the meaning of a literary text between languages, the translator must make a raft of decisions that ultimately inflect the way in which the translated text can be read. Put simply, the translator chooses the way in which she navigates between languages, and in this choice acts more like the author of the text than a mere passive conduit for the passage of meaning between languages. In other words, the role of the translator is not mechanical; it is creative.

This observation about the necessarily creative aspect of translation, though, tells us something rather important: every translation must change in some way the nature of the object being translated because it is impossible to know (and therefore represent) such an object (literary or otherwise) in its entirety. That is to say, we can never get to a point where we know every dimension and quality of an object, and as such there will always be something about the object that escapes our translation. This is what the literary translator experiences when she sees her translation pulled in two competing directions – towards literal fidelity on the one hand and cultural/contextual fidelity on the other. There will always be some dimension of a text that goes untranslated. For this reason the seasoned translator knows to abandon at the very beginning of the translation process any hope of producing an absolutely faithful iteration of the original material. Literary translation teaches us, then, that we can never give a full account of an object under translation. That is to say, if we adopt a different kind of language, no act of translation can ever "exhaust" its object.

Significantly, Graham Harman maintains that every encounter that we have with the world – in fact every encounter or relation that any entity has with any other entity – is an act of translation. As such, our encounter with the world must also be characterized as one of distortion or transformation. Since the world has a subterranean reality that cannot be regarded (Kant's noumenal plane of reality), Harman says that we must translate our encounters with the world into a form that then allows us to make sense of them. This, then, is the function of language – it is the means by which we translate our encounter(s) with the world. But Harman's assertion takes us further than this simple observation. In the same way that language is a translation of our experience of the world, so too are the very experiences that we try to capture in language! In fact, every encounter with the world that we seek to understand (whether linguistic in nature or not) is a product of an act of translation that cannot, as an implicit function of the act of translation itself, render the world in its full definition. As Harman writes, "direct knowledge of anything is impossible," and that is because "to be truly direct, knowledge of a thing would have to be that thing itself" (2013, 30).

It is because of this gap that develops between an object and our translation of it that we must maintain a sense that our theories about the world can only ever grant an imperfect account of things. However, I think it is important to make clear at this point that although we are led to acknowledge the imperfect character of human thought here, this is not at all the same as saying that our knowledge of the world cannot be trusted as it is. Rather, a belief in a perpetual gap between noumenal and phenomenal realities reduces to the observation that our imperfect knowledge always leaves room for the possibility of a finer understanding of things. Let me take gravity as my example here. We have known for a very long time that gravity exists and that it works in a very particular way. In fact, we are so knowledgeable about gravity that we can predict the movement of various celestial bodies, recognize the way in which light responds to it, and describe its effect on natural convection. In 1969, Neil Armstrong and Buzz Aldrin walked on the moon because of our understanding of gravity. Yet, if we put all of this to one side for a moment, we must admit to ourselves that we still do not really know what gravity *is*. Scientists continue to debate amongst themselves whether or not the experimental data shows gravity to be a force powered by ghostly graviton particles, or an effect of mass on space-time, or a force peeking through into our universe from another universe or dimension. The point here is not to demonstrate our level of ignorance about gravity, but rather to make clear the fact that even without a *full* understanding of something we can know enough to make an idea or concept do (some extremely sophisticated) work for us. Who would bet against our current scientific ideas being refined over the years to come? This, then, is all that the speculative realist claims when she asserts that all human knowledge is imperfect.

The consequence of living in a world of the gaps that open up between noumenal and phenomenal realities is that we are fated to live a life of uncertainty. However, this is not for the same reasons that Edmund Husserl and the other phenomenologists suggested. Indeed, the second response that the speculative realist might give to the anti-realist insistence that a truly mind-independent world makes any representation of it unreliable is that a world of things eventually does impose itself on us. For the speculative realist, the aesthetic plane that the phenomenologists followed all the way down to its most fundamental unit is one that eventually runs up against the world as it is. The importance of this observation is that, contrary to what one might initially think, a world of things preserves an atmosphere of epistemic unreliability that gives way under the incessant circulation of aesthetics demanded by phenomenology. It is Timothy Morton who gives the logic of such an idea in his essay on poetry: "If reality were aesthetic all the way down," he writes, "then we would *know* it was 'just' an illusion and its power to beguile us would disappear" (Morton 2012, 213). That is to say, the fact that we can speculate on a world of things operating underneath the domain of the aesthetic, for all the ontological stability that such a claim seems to offer, means that we can never know with certainty either that the phenomenal plane is all there is *or* that it eventually resolves to touch the noumenal. In this way, the very act of speculating about the world as it is preserves our life of uncertainty.

Yet, despite living in an uncertain world, the speculative realist enjoys life in just the same way that we all do, for the fact of the matter is that such uncertainty in no way impedes the ability to live a life. In fact, we could argue quite strongly that it encourages a more vigorous engagement with life. Clearly, an awareness of the discursive and therefore literally fabricated nature of the aesthetic plane means that everything within this horizon is ripe for re-negotiation and re-evaluation – social structures, morality, the rule of law, economic systems, to name just a few. In short, because the speculative realist is willing to acknowledge the limitations of our constructed understanding of the world, it almost becomes a responsibility to think again about the ways in which we live and the seemingly naturalized structures that make possible our life as socialized beings.

Those who have some familiarity with contemporary literary theory will detect more than a fleeting association here between this description of the speculative realist and the poststructuralist. Indeed, both understand the inherent discursive nature of the way in which we build our knowledge of the world, and both take this as a challenge to the individual to take responsibility for their own structures of knowing. But it is the way in which the speculative realist maintains that the "real world" constantly bursts through layers of discursivity in order to impose itself on the human world that shows the sharp division between the two positions. For the speculative realist, one cannot debate the fact that gravity exists. We can certainly debate the name that we give to the phenomenon and we can debate its natural character, but we cannot debate the fact that the result of leaving your second-floor apartment by the window rather than the door will always end unpleasantly for you. Similarly, one cannot debate the fact that the climate, regardless of whether we are cognizant of it or not, profoundly influences our lives. Likewise, it is clear that our immediate environment radically impacts on the kind of (human) activities that can take place there. History, for example, has taught us well that the most prosperous cities emerge from a very particular assemblage of geographical features. Although the speculative realist must admit that we will never be in a position to fully understand such things, it is nonetheless clear that this world that acts regardless of our ability to perceive it has shaped (and continues to shape) in profound ways the human account of the world.

Importantly, it is this observation that highlights what is perhaps the singular endeavor of all the various programs of research brought together under the umbrella of speculative realism – *to speculate on the character of a world that (we can never know but nonetheless) influences every aspect of human existence and thought*. But, that being said, we must also acknowledge that it is this call to speculate that sits at the heart of most of the concerns expressed about this return to an object-oriented philosophy and a mind-independent reality. To be sure, the activity of speculation recalls images of a pre-critical thought that plucks hypotheses from the ether and plays a game of assertion that long ago abandoned the need for evidence or justification. Yet, the activity of speculation that is embedded in speculative realism is not this kind of outright rejection of critical advances. As Levi Bryant makes clear:

Instead, it comes from a recognition of their inherent limitations. Speculation in this sense aims at something "beyond"
the critical and linguistic turns. As such, it recuperates the pre-
critical sense of "speculation" as a concern with the Absolute,
while also taking into account the undeniable progress that is
due to the labor of critique. (Bryant et al 2011, 3)

The point is that we need to be very careful about how we think
of the act of speculation if we are to award it any kind of legit-
imacy as a means by which we can come to navigate the world.
That is to say, we cannot be satisfied with the (common) species
of speculation that seeks to bend our experience of the world of
things to an initial belief that refuses to open itself up to
amendment. Such speculation can only result in dogma – a set of
principles regarded by those who put them in place as incontro-
vertibly true. To accept this kind of speculation is in fact to
champion a willful ignorance of what we can discern (and have
already discerned) about the world. And that will get us
nowhere.

For this reason, the kind of speculation in which the speculative realist must take part cannot be one based on mere whim.
Instead, it must be the kind of speculation that is derived from a
belief or idea that one is willing to abandon or at least radically
revise if the world seems to tell us something different about
itself. Donald Verene gets it right then when he writes in defense
of speculative philosophy that "to speculate is not to speak in a
fanciful way or to think in an unfounded way apart from
experience." He continues, "To speculate [...] is to attempt to
meditate and narrate the whole of things in a way that satisfies
reason in its connection with sense, imagination, and memory"
(2009, x). Understood in this way, speculation is not a flight of
fancy or any other whimsical attempt to escape the harsh reality
of the world. Rather, it is an attempt to re-acknowledge the
significant role that the imagination plays in building our

rational interpretation of the world. To this extent, it is worth paying attention to what the English mathematician and philosopher Alfred North Whitehead had to say about the importance of the act of speculation in his book *Process and Reality* (1929). Critiquing the cold inductive reasoning of Francis Bacon, which is to say the way of thinking that began scientific method, Whitehead writes:

What Bacon omitted was the play of a free imagination, controlled by the requirements of coherence and logic. The true method of discovery is like the flight of an aeroplane. It starts from the ground of particular observation; it makes a flight in the thin air of imaginative generalization; and it again lands for renewed observation rendered acute by rational interpretation. (1985, 5)

Speculation, Whitehead makes clear, is not unscientific. In fact, it is the very means by which scientific advances are made. We observe the phenomenal world, speculate on the noumenal world beneath it, and in the knowledge that anything we can say about the world is necessarily imperfect because it is an act of translation, we are nonetheless led into genuinely unanticipated and genuinely new areas of thought.

This, then, is how we should read the breakthrough work of the great Austrian physicist Ludwig Boltzmann, who at the end of the nineteenth century showed that if we peer at any object closely enough we must ultimately abandon certainty for probability. At the level of the miniscule, Boltzmann revealed that we lose the ability to say *exactly* where any atom stands at any particular point in time. The sheer number of atoms in a gas contained in a test tube, for example, makes it impossible to say with any kind of meaningful accuracy where any particular atom is at any particular time. The best we can ever do, Boltzmann suggested, is give a probability for where any atom might be at any time. It sounds so obvious to today's ears, but it was a revolutionary assertion not least for the fact that it posited atoms at a time when they had still not been proven to exist! Nonetheless, the scientific community would eventually come to agree with Boltzmann and in so doing overturn physics as something fixated on certainty. Boltzmann's statistical mechanics would become a powerful analytical tool for thermodynamic systems, and psychologically it would pave the way for the scientific community's acceptance of the even-more-confrontational findings of quantum physics. In this way, then, Boltzmann speculated on the existence of atoms and the way in which they acted as a gas, and in so doing arrived at a revolutionary new way of thinking about and describing the world.

For the French philosopher Gilles Deleuze and his long-time writing partner Félix Guattari, the process of enquiry outlined by Whitehead and pursued by Boltzmann actually equates to doing philosophy "properly." For them, philosophy is less about describing the thought of others and more about forming and testing new ways of thinking about the world in which we live. "Philosophy," they explain, "is the art of forming, inventing, and fabricating concepts" (1994, 2). That is all. Yet, the ramifications of this simple assertion are quite remarkable. Understood like this, speculation brings philosophy to science, to the extent that it interrupts the processes and patterns that science looks to organize by thinking about the moments at which a particular system changes and becomes something new. Of course, that is not to say that scientists have never reflected on or contemplated their own discoveries. As Deleuze and Guattari make clear, "Mathematicians, as mathematicians, have never waited for philosophers before reflecting on mathematics" (1994, 6). But such reflection, contemplation, or even communication is not, according to Deleuze and Guattari, the domain of philosophy. Philosophy is in the business of creating concepts, and this mode of invention is intimately linked to the act of speculation.

If the world of the twentieth century and beyond can only be "understood" to the extent that we can draw a "line of best fit" through the range of experiences and scientific observations that we have translated into meaning, then the speculative realist would insist that it is our duty to speculate on the character of the world as it is. And that is indeed what we have seen in recent years coming from various science departments across the world – speculations premised on careful scientific observations that result in seemingly preposterous or outrageous suggestions about the material reality of the world in which we live: the holographic universe, the simulation hypothesis, or the many-worlds interpretation, for example.[3] Each one of these hypotheses is an excellent example of the way in which Whitehead saw science progressing – given what we can reliably say of the world, what kind of speculation can we make and go on to test? Undoubtedly, some of the more outlandish hypotheses currently circulating in physics departments will be proven to be incorrect, but in understanding why something cannot be possible we of course also learn something new and therefore valuable about the world.

What, then, has all this to do with literature? Well, for the literary critic who takes seriously the basic tenets of speculative realism there is much to take away from this discussion. First is to embrace the fact that language simply cannot apprehend the world as it is. Regardless of any claims made to the contrary, language must be construed as something that ultimately distorts or modifies the *noumenal* world. For this reason, the literature that emerges through our language must always be thought of as an imperfect rendition of the world – especially if its explicit claim is to capture the world "as it is," which has always been the claim of literary realism. In light of this, it seems better to think of literature solely in terms of an exercise in aesthetics, which is to say as a form of expression that interrogates the gaps that open up between the world and our image or experience of that same world. However, just to be clear, in the same way that our previous discussion of gravity showed that a lack of ontological knowledge does not necessarily impede the sophisticated way in which we can use critical concepts, the assertion of literature as a purely aesthetic form is not to insist that it is an ephemeral or inconsequential phenomenon. As we all know, literature can profoundly affect the way in which the reader thinks and behaves, and to this extent it has an important part to play in any consideration of the political or the social.

The second significant observation to highlight for the literary critic is the consequence that such an inability to know the world has on meaning. If we cannot know the world, as the object-oriented speculative realists would maintain, then the search for meaning within or around a literary text can only be regarded as a fool's errand. At best, meaning is something that can be said to take place upon the plane of discursivity. But it can go no further. It cannot, for example, be drawn from this plane of human devising and be used to somehow understand better the noumenal world. Understood like this, meaning is both a product of and bound by the reach of a particular sign-system. Without the sense of an objective meaning that can be grasped through rigorous textual examination, the job of the literary critic necessarily becomes something quite different to that which it had always been supposed to be. It can no longer be the job of the literary critic to assert what a text means. Rather, it must be the job of the literary critic to speculate on the literary text. That is to say, it is the job of the literary critic to become a (Deleuzian) philosopher – to speculate on a text in a way that results in the invention of new concepts or new ways of talking about the world. In the spirit of the work of Deleuze and Guattari, it is to produce concepts that will take us beyond our habits of perception and into a condition that allows for the creation of "the new."

If this sounds like a dramatic departure for the industry of literary criticism, that is because to some extent it is. But let us be clear: such consciously inventive criticism is not without precedent. The problem for the literary critic is that he commonly has to look beyond the field of *literary* criticism in order to find examples of such. To this end then, let us turn to the field of psychoanalysis. How better to think of Sigmund Freud's reading of Sophocles's play *Oedipus Rex* than as the invention of a new concept by which to rethink our understanding of human nature? In *The Interpretation of Dreams* (1899), Freud reads the plight of Oedipus as the externalization of a psychological phenomenon that is innate to all human beings. That is to say, Freud reads a play, and creates from it a concept – the Oedipus complex – that he will then go on to employ as a new tool by which to interrogate and understand human psychosexual behaviors. Here, the Sigmund Freud who we have always been taught to call a "neurologist" or a "psychiatrist" reveals himself to be something more like a Deleuzian philosopher and, at the same time, a speculative-realist literary critic.

Similarly, the literary work of the Marquis de Sade and Leopold von Sacher-Masoch has been read in this concept-creative way. The noted Austrian psychiatrist Richard von Krafft-Ebing read both de Sade's and Sacher-Masoch's writing in a way that allowed him to organize two "new" kinds of psychopathology – sadism and masochism. Talking of how he came to term these new psychopathologies in his book *Psychopathia Sexualis* (1886), Krafft-Ebing writes of masochism:

I feel justified in calling this sexual anomaly "Masochism," because the author Sacher-Masoch frequently made this perversion, which up to his time was quite unknown to the scientific world as such, the substratum of his writings. (1939, 132)

Again, this is nothing other than the literary criticism of the speculative realist. Here, Krafft-Ebing interrogates the "substratum" of

Sacher-Masoch's writing and finds there something that becomes a concept or device by which to think again about the (human) world.

Even though the substance of the examples given here are different, they both demonstrate the fact that the literatures with which they deal are primary spaces of speculation. This is not because the literary text is somehow unreal or artificial or indulges in flights of fancy, but rather because it gestures inevitably towards a reality that lies somewhere beyond the one of which we are cognizant. For this reason alone, literature cannot be thought of as a simple reflection of the world. Yet, neither can it be said to function independently of it. Here, literature alludes to an inscrutable reality that lies behind or beneath its composition, and as Graham Harman writes, this structure of *allure* "is the key phenomenon of all the arts" (2012, 187). Literature alludes to the fact that there is another presence elsewhere, a "real world" that it can never capture fully, and as it does so it reveals itself to be an important space in which we constantly map our self-conscious speculations about the world as we think it.

This idea can be put another way: literature has been playing a game with us for a very long time – a game whose rules follow the logic of the material conditional. The proposition of all literature is "*If x* is (not) part of the world, *then* the world would look like *y*." We see this in the writing of Charles Dickens as much as we do in, say, Sophocles or Thomas Pynchon. But nowhere is this observation more nakedly apparent than in the genre of speculative fiction, for the fact is that this form of writing deals most directly and obviously with the seminal question, "what if...?"

Indeed, playing the game of the material conditional is exactly how the celebrated American science-fiction writer Ray Bradbury conceived his novels and short stories. "Science fiction is any idea that occurs in the head and doesn't exist yet, but soon will," Bradbury explained in a late interview with Sam Weller.

"As soon as you have an idea that changes some small part of the world," he continues, "you are writing science fiction" (Weller 2010). That is to say, you are writing (science) fiction precisely at the moment you speculate about the character of another possible world that comes into being when one value or term is removed, added, or altered in some way from the world in which we participate. Take for example Bradbury's modern classic novel, *Fahrenheit 451* (1953). For Bradbury, this novel emerges from reasoning out the consequences of just one seemingly minor change to our own world – that the State has banned all books. Given this material condition, Bradbury asks in his novel, what would a contemporary American society look like? And of course, the answer is: not very pretty. His vision of a world without books is one of intellectual decrepitude and terrible depression in the masses; participatory "entertainment" piped remorselessly into homes by way of televisions as large as walls in order to distract people from the mindless drudgery of a life without enquiry. In this world, curiosity dies and those who attempt to live another kind of life either become savage ascetics or are branded mentally ill and institutionalized.

The rightly lauded English novelist J.G. Ballard saw this early work of Bradbury as something very special. To Ballard, it was immediately clear that *Fahrenheit 451* was strikingly different to the other kinds of "science fiction" that were populating the book stands of the 1950s. Here was a science-fiction novel that demonstrated perfectly Ballard's sense that the proper subject matter for the literature of the future (that is to say, Ballard's kind of "science fiction") was not "space, interstellar travel, extra-terrestrial life forms, and galactic wars" (1962, 117), but rather the world of "everyday life." Modernity and the way in which it was seemingly estranging the very people it was supposed to be emancipating from the rigors of a hard-fought life was uppermost in Ballard's mind, and it is this that he saw at play in Bradbury's *Fahrenheit 451*. Turning the gaze of the science-fiction writer inward, from the cosmos to what Ballard called the "inner space" of the human mind, Bradbury had responded *avant la lettre* to Ballard's call for science fiction to become a "speculative poetry" – which is to say, a literature that consciously engages with:

> more psycho-literary ideas, more meta-biological and meta-chemical concepts, private time-systems, synthetic psychologies and space-times, more of the sombre half-worlds one glimpses in the paintings of schizophrenics, all in all a complete speculative poetry and fantasy of science. (Ballard 1996, 198)

Somewhat regardless of whether we eventually come to call Bradbury's *Fahrenheit 451* a work of speculative fiction or science fiction – and for the record, I think it is better positioned and read as speculative fiction – the point for us to dwell on here is that *all* fiction takes genesis from this initial act of speculation. Clearly, Bradbury's and Ballard's writing engages this speculation more explicitly than other works of literature, but it is true to say that *every* genre of fiction arises from contemplating the consequences of a material-conditional proposition. Put simply, in this regard, Bradbury and Ballard are no different to Shakespeare or Scott Fitzgerald.

We have covered a lot of ground in this chapter so it is perhaps wise to conclude by recalling some of the significant assertions that have been made. First is the observation that every object translates the encounters it has with the world in its own way. Importantly, if we agree with this observation then we must also agree that the noumenal world will always remain "other" to us. Indeed, we can have no direct access to it for the simple fact is that we can never interrogate and understand it on its own terms. Since meaning is the product of a knowledge that can only ever be incomplete, our second important observation to make is that we must give up on our search for meaning. Such a search is revealed to be a wild goose chase. In the absence of the search for meaning we must turn our attention elsewhere. Speculative realism suggests that we should learn to once again speculate on the character of a world that we can never fully know. As we have seen, science speculates on the world in this way, as does philosophy, as does literature. The reason why we read literature as an expression of such speculation is that it always alludes to an "other" world that is tantalizingly beyond our reach. And in the same way that we can never hope to know the world, the literary critic can never hope to know or recount the full meaning of a literary text. Given this, the literary critic must become more like a (Deleuzian) philosopher than a traditional literary critic. That is to say, the new job of the literary critic is not to discern the meaning of a literary text but rather to speculate on the text in such a way that new concepts emerge – concepts that can give us a different way of looking at and thinking about the world.

Literary (French) Symbolism

Although speculative fiction plays the game of the material conditional more nakedly than any other genre, it is perhaps the poetry of the French Symbolists that has explored most explicitly the Kantian tension between word and world. Symbolism arose in the middle of the nineteenth century in France as both an aggressive reaction to literary Realism and a growing unease with the inability of Romanticism to get to grips with what some thought of as the failure of aesthetics. Whereas the practitioners of Realism had always claimed to capture the world "as it is," the Symbolist poets – most notably Charles Baudelaire, Arthur Rimbaud, Stéphane Mallarmé, and Paul Verlaine – concluded in their own ways that to know the world one must look at it "sideways." That is to say, this group of poets distrusted entirely the idea that one could gain access to the world by direct inter-rogation. For these men, language could do little more than suggest the presence of a world that itself only "spoke" in symbol and metaphor. While this sense of things was largely shared by the Romantic poets, who expressed it through a pervasive mood of gloaming that we now think of as a defining characteristic of the Romantic period, for the Symbolists it was this human failure to directly touch the Real that would become their subject matter. The rather simple question that every Symbolist poet asked himself was, "How do I access the Real? How do I write of the real world?" But while the question may have been an easy one to ask, the answers it elicited were devil-ishly complex and difficult to follow.

Nonetheless, it is the answer to this question of literary repre-sentation arrived at by Charles Baudelaire and Stéphane Mallarmé with which this chapter is concerned. Not because these writers were successful in finding a way of talking about the noumenal world, but because they were not. The detours and dead-ends that these poets ran up against as they put their (linguistic) experiments in place in order to try and touch the Real are something of which the speculative-realist critic should be especially conscious. For, what these dead-ends show us is that although this literary movement was perhaps the first to exclusively concern itself with a mind-independent world of things that refuses human enquiry (and therefore the first to stake a claim as *la littérature exemplaire* of speculative realism), the conclusions it reached were nothing short of anathema to the concerns of object-oriented philosophy. In other words, literary Symbolism shows again that a shared commitment to the autonomy of reality is no guarantee of sympathy with the intent to return objectivity to objects.

Let us begin, though, with the Francophile Greek poet and essayist Jean Moréas who marked out the practices and concerns of literary Symbolism in the French newspaper *Le Figaro* and in so doing gave the literary movement its name. On 18 September 1886, Moréas penned an article titled "Le Symbolisme," which today stands as something of a manifesto for the Symbolist movement. Having made mention of the pedigree of the ideas that underscored the work of poets such as Charles Baudelaire, Stéphane Mallarmé, and Paul Verlaine, Moréas went on to give an explicit account of what he thought of as the only kind of writing that could emerge from such thought:

Enemy of teaching, declamation, false sensibility, and objective description, the Symbolist poets seek to clothe the Idea in a sensuous form, which, nevertheless, would not be an end in itself, but which would help to express the Idea, whilst remaining subject to it. The Idea, in its turn, must not let itself be deprived of the sumptuous robes of external analogies; for the essential character of Symbolist art consists in never trying to reproduce the Idea in itself. In this art form, therefore, depictions of nature, human actions, indeed all concrete phenomena should not show themselves as such: they are outward forms, whose purpose is to represent their hidden affinities with primordial Ideas. (Travers 2001, 148)

This is an especially rich passage from Moréas's manifesto that cuts to the very heart of the interests of the Symbolist writers. First is Moréas's observation that Symbolism engages fully with the principle of Platonic Forms (the Ideal). And second is the implication that such a direct engagement with Platonic Forms is an inevitable consequence of an inability to gain direct "access" to the "real world" (or the noumenal world). It is worth dwelling on these points a little in order to understand better the character of literary Symbolism.

If there is one thing that the non-philosopher associates with Plato it is the notion of "Platonic Forms" or "the Platonic Ideal." Through the course of his writings, Plato advocated the idea that the world that appears to our senses is in some way an impoverished version of a more real and perfect realm. In this perfect realm, "forms" or "ideas" are not only eternal (for the fact is that they cannot change because they are already "perfect"), but also vital to the structure and character of our world. So it is that all the chairs that one might actually sit on are fundamentally impoverished versions of an Ideal chair that exists "elsewhere." The same is of course true for tables, trees, turnips, and, importantly, thoughts. The point is that any form or thought that we can actually experience is never anything more than an imperfect realization of a perfect state of things that exists beyond the material world. In other words, every object or idea that we encounter is necessarily in a perpetual state of "becoming real" since no object or idea in this world can ever claim to be more than tending towards the (impossible) condition of the Ideal. Moreover, because our world can never become this realm of the

Ideal, it is clear that we are fated to live in and experience an intrinsically flawed life that immediately prohibits our access to the truth of things. If we agree with Plato, not only must we acknowledge that the world we seek to interrogate is defective (and therefore cannot be a route to "truth"), we must also conclude that our speculations or thoughts about the world are faulty even before we begin! In short, Platonic Forms inexorably short-circuit any claim that we can make to interrogate the world directly.

Now, if the world is to be understood like this then the truth of things must necessarily lie in the inaccessible realm of perfection that we have learned to call the Platonic Ideal. Nonetheless, the task that the Symbolist poets set themselves was to try and touch this realm of the perfect. In order to do so, they recognized that they could not confront the world in a direct manner. What was called for was a way of thinking and writing that worked by association, analogy, inference, implication, and affinity – a literature, that is, of the symbol which could gesture towards the Ideal state of things and therefore the truth of the world.

To this end, it is important to consider Baudelaire's assertion that the Ideal towards which he and others reached through poetry was not some fantastical abstraction but rather a tangible form that one could ultimately grasp. In his much-read *Salon de 1846*, Baudelaire writes, "the ideal is not that vague thing, that boring and intangible dream floating on the ceilings of academies; an ideal is the individual modified by the individual, rebuilt and restored by brush or chisel to the dazzling truth of its own essential harmony" (1995, 78). Here, the Ideal exists even if it is something that ultimately arises from our negotiation with the world. But if it does exist in this way – which is to say as more than just a moment of intellectual fancy – as Baudelaire seems to be saying here, then the startling natural conclusion to be made is that one must be able to eventually

34

touch it. Such is the conclusion that drives Baudelaire's poetic output.

Perhaps Baudelaire's best-known attempt to "touch the Ideal" in this way is his poem "Correspondances" from his infamous collection of poems, *Fleurs du Mal* (*Flowers of Evil*).[4] The opening quatrain reads:

Nature is a temple in which living pillars
Sometimes give voice to confused words;
Man passes there through forests of symbols
Which look at him with understanding eyes.

From the beginning then, Baudelaire is thinking of the world in terms of symbols, or what Plato called "images of a divine copy." The world in which we walk here only gestures towards the existence of the invisible, higher reality of the Ideal. But in the next quatrain we get an introduction to the way in which Baudelaire attempts to describe the "forests of symbols" that constitutes our world:

Like prolonged echoes mingling in the distance
In a deep and tenebrous unity,
Vast as the dark of night and as the light of day,
Perfumes, sounds, and colors correspond.

It is important to note the last line of this quatrain, where Baudelaire begins to bring together our sensual account of the world. Here, the olfactory, the auditory, and the visual come into some kind of correspondence with each other in order to describe "Nature." But it is regarding the way in which these senses talk across one another in the final tercets of the poem that one begins to understand the value that Baudelaire gives to these synesthetic moments:

There are perfumes as cool as the flesh of children,
Sweet as oboes, green as meadows
– And others are corrupt, and rich, triumphant,

With power to expand into infinity,
Like amber and incense, musk, benzoin,
That sing the ecstasy of the soul and senses.

One might not care for some of the terms that Baudelaire brings into association here ("perfumes as cool as the flesh of children," for example), but the fact is that writing of the perfume of the world in terms of our sense of touch ("perfumes as cool as"), and our sense of taste ("Sweet as oboes" – sweet as oboes!?), and our understanding of color ("green as meadows"), and of our ingrained ideas about morality and elation ("others are corrupt, and rich, triumphant") suggests a certain feeling or mood that we are encouraged to reflect on towards the infinite ("With power to expand into infinity"). Of course, what Baudelaire says here of the fragrances that are an undeniable quality of the world in which we live can be reimagined and repeated for both the "sounds and colors" that we encounter. What aromas would the blue of the sky suggest or the gold of the autumn forest?

For Baudelaire, all of our senses can be brought together in this way in order to recreate a landscape of rich sensations that ultimately evokes a pre-linguistic experience of the world. Put another way, Baudelaire creates his own symbols of the world ("perfumes [...] sweet as oboes") "whose purpose," to quote Moréas again, "is to represent their hidden affinities with primordial Ideas." That is to say, it is not that the symbol is supposed to be the representation of a thing or idea, but rather that the symbol inaugurates an implicit (and therefore "purer") association with an object or an idea. Take for example the tiger and its relationship to strength. Because one of its obvious qualities is the power to bring large prey to the ground, some think of the tiger as a *representation* of the quality of strength. Understood as such, the animal serves merely as a vessel – it becomes that which simply suggests something else. However, understood as a symbol of strength, the animal becomes the very embodiment of strength. Strength is not elsewhere and represented through the tiger; strength *is* the tiger. In this way, the tiger and the idea of strength become intimately linked – a structured affinity that (it is hoped) gets us closer to the Ideal of strength. In other words, Baudelaire's "perfumes as cool as the flesh of children" is supposed to get us closer to Nature; it is supposed to invoke a purer sense of the world than we can achieve by simply employing descriptive language.

One consequence of thinking about symbols in this way is that although they gesture towards the world as it is, ultimately they function to divorce our language from the world. In getting us to think in an analogous way about a world of things, language talks only to language and the noumenal world slips by, unregarded. Recognizing that the world withdraws under the impress of language, Baudelaire made clear that the poet must once and for all forsake the idea of trying to describe the world as it is. In its place, the poet must instead concentrate on the affective resonance of language and the concepts and ideas to which it gives birth. Put simply, Baudelaire makes a case for the Platonic Ideal and not the world itself (or even as it appears to be) as the engine of poetry. The point is made perfectly clear in his later poem "Paysage," in which, gazing out over a city that one presumes to be Paris, he writes:

And when winter comes with its monotonous snow,
I shall close all the shutters and draw all the drapes
So I can build at night my fairy palaces.
Then I shall dream of pale blue horizons, gardens,
Fountains weeping into alabaster basins,
Of kisses, of birds singing morning and evening,

And of all that is most childlike in the Idyll.
Riot, storming vainly at my window,
Will not make me raise my head from my desk,
For I shall be plunged in the voluptuousness
Of evoking the Springtime with my will alone

It is tempting to think of the Ideal as just a means to escape the world here, but it is more than that. In this poem, Baudelaire makes clear that all one ever really needs in order to think about the world is the Ideal. After all, the images that we can manufacture in order to strike an affinity to the Ideal can be produced, he says here, by "will alone." Indeed, it is also by will alone that we are able to fabricate an image of the world that will ultimately come to color our sense of our past and, because of that, our future. Understood like this, what Baudelaire is saying in these lines is something rather profound – although it may look as though it is the world that gives us our ideas, it is in fact our own imagination. That is to say, it is our mind that makes manifest the ideas and objects by which we will attempt to render the unknowable world knowable. To this end, Peter Nicholls gets it right when he concludes that Baudelaire's poetry "predicts the psychological (or interior) landscape of the Symbolists, the natural setting of the poem no longer an ordinary, external one, but rather a zone of the mind where objects pulse with the same inner vibration" (1995, 26).[5] For Baudelaire, it is the mind that organizes the world; it is the mind that is the most important actor in the search for the Real.

Mallarmé, too, was intrigued by the Ideal. Indeed, the same principal theme of Baudelaire's work emerges in that of Mallarmé – the poet's longing to turn his back on the harsh world of reality and to seek refuge in an ideal world. But whereas Baudelaire explored the disjunction between word and world with vigor, Mallarmé became haunted by his inability to make language grasp the essential reality of things. In short, Mallarmé recognized that language could only fail him. What a desperate position for a poet to find himself in! And it is this desperation that one sees at the opening of one his most quoted poems, "The Sky" (1864):

The serene irony of the eternal Sky
Depresses, with the indolence of flowers,
The impotent poet cursing poetry
Across a sterile waste of leaden Hours.

Of course, the irony to which Mallarmé refers here concerns the fact that even this most quotidian of things, the sky, easily evades his attempts to describe it in any kind of meaningful way. To grasp the essential character or quality of this thing that we see every day (even if we do not think about it every day) was too much for Mallarmé – not because he did not have the words at his disposal to capture the character of the sky, but because he was beginning to realize that descriptive language itself could not give entryway to the essential reality of an object. So, Mallarmé concludes his poem by raging, "*I am haunted. The sky! The sky! The sky! The sky!*"

For Mallarmé, the problem of knowing the world – that is, of gaining access to it, of creating meaning – is that our language is not fit for such a purpose. He writes in one of his prose pieces, "Languages are imperfect because multiple; the supreme language is missing […] the diversity of languages on earth means that no one can utter words which would bear the miraculous stamp of Truth Herself Incarnate" (qtd. in Kwasny 2004, 154). It is a suspicion that enjoys an extremely long intellectual history and one that of course takes us back to the Biblical toppling of the tower of Babel. In the book of Genesis, we are told that what allowed the men of earth to build a tower that threatened to reach heaven itself was the fact that "the whole earth was of one language, and of one speech" (11: 1).[6] The implication here is that this shared language of men was the first

39

human language – the language by which Adam became Nomothete, the name-giver to all the animals of Creation (2: 19). While it is not at all clear on what basis Adam actually chose the names he gave to the animals – "either he gave them the names that, by some extra-linguistic right, were already due to them, or he gave them those names we still use on the basis of a convention initiated by Adam" (Eco 1999, 24) – the suspicion of those who lament the confounding of this first human language is that it is the only language that has ever promised access to the fundamental truth about the world as it is.[7]

It is unsurprising then to learn of the vast number of attempts that thinkers have made over the centuries to either recreate the Adamic language – such as the attempts made by Raymond Lully, Gottfried Leibniz, and others to fabricate a rational language of perfection – or to rediscover the lost language. For, the prize of recovering the Biblical first language is the chance to know again the absolute nature of the world. But even though every such endeavor has failed in its aim, each one has taught us something significant about the character of the languages we have today. The proliferation of languages that we see today for example, teaches us that our linguistic relationship to the world is entirely arbitrary. And this is what Mallarmé understood, and what led him to his frustration with language. The mere fact that an object can be represented in a number of different languages – the object known as a *tree* is also known as *arbre* (French), *baum* (German), *mti* (Swahili), *igi* (Yoruba), and so on – evidences the point. No language can claim a perfect relationship between word and world, and for Mallarmé that meant that the Truth that was said to reside in the Ideal was already lost to language.

It would take years of suffering frustration upon frustration, of watching language fail to fulfill its promise as a means of knowing and talking about the world, before Mallarmé began to think in a different way about language and poetry. Cautiously and carefully, Mallarmé began to think of poetry itself as a kind of compensation for the loss of Truth in language. What had so perplexed Mallarmé was the way in which language seemed to simply replace rather than represent or symbolize the object it was employed to name. For this reason, Mallarmé thought of language as inherently destructive by nature. Even though one wrote or spoke in order to express something, all that could ever result from such an expression was the image and resonance of language itself and the void of the Real that it left behind. But it was when Mallarmé finally realized that this destructive power of language could also promise transcendence that everything changed. Years later, Mallarmé began to reflect on the fact that even though the word acted as a substitute for the world itself, the word as captured in poetry *did* manage to express some kind of meaning. Given that it did so, Mallarmé recognized that in some sense poetic language triumphed over the world. That is to say, he recognized that poetic language created its own reality.

Importantly, since this literary-linguistic reality had no need to travel first through the representation of the world in order to make sense, Mallarmé concluded that poetic language was much closer to the Ideal than that of our day-to-day language. In making a case for pursuing this poetic language through a literature of the symbol, Mallarmé asked:

Why should we perform the miracle by which a natural object is almost made to disappear beneath the magic waving wand of the written word, if not to divorce that object from the direct and palpable, and so conjure up its essence in all purity? (qtd. in Kwasny 2004, 156)

"Out of a number of words," he continued, "poetry fashions a single new word which is total in itself and foreign to the language – a kind of incantation" (qtd. in Kwasny 2004, 159). This is an important statement because it not only makes clear the difference between poetic language and our language of the everyday; it also makes clear that Mallarmé thought of poetry as that which could capture the essence of an object purely because poetic language divorced the idea of the object from the physical being of the object. Indeed, it was this that stood at the heart of what was to become the great Mallarméan dictum – *from a language that inaugurates the void of the Real as it usurps its object of representation, a moment of creation emerges.* The sentiment is perhaps expressed most clearly in his well-known assertion, "Destruction was my Beatrice" (qtd. in Lloyd 1988, 77). From the negation instructed by language, Mallarmé sees here the possibility that gives birth to poetry.

So, the Mallarméan account of the world is a fairly complicated one that develops from the observation that from destruction emerges that which is new to the world. Language ultimately destroys the world for it can only describe a void, but it also lets loose a new creation. This then is not about accessing the world through writing of the impressions that are made by material objects, which Mallarmé would come to call "borrowed impressions"; it is about becoming truly creative – inventing the idea of an object rather than simply reporting the representation of the object as a particular concrete thing. As such, for Mallarmé the object of poetry was not reality as such (our access to the noumenal world), but rather the "pure notion" or "Ideal" that invests it. And that, Mallarmé maintained, could only be got at indirectly through the suggestiveness of the symbol.

There are then both clear lines of similarity and division between the Symbolist and speculative-realist positions. Even though the speculative realists would agree that the world can only be got at indirectly, they nonetheless would refuse to follow Baudelaire and Mallarmé towards the Platonic Ideal and the centrality of the human experience that it implies. Why? Because to coddle the Ideal in the way demonstrated by the Symbolist poets would be to reinstate the very correlation between world and mind that speculative realism in each of its guises unites to

42

confront. If we are to claim that a world of objects exists independently of our ability to perceive it, then it is absolutely necessary
to refuse to entertain the notion that the Ideal structures our
experience of the world.

This then is why Graham Harman attempts to go beyond the
discipline of phenomenology with his object-oriented
philosophy. Just like literary Symbolism, phenomenology parti-
tions the world in a Kantian fashion (along the fissure between
noumenal and phenomenal realities) so that it can concentrate on
our subjective experience of the phenomena of the world. And
just like literary Symbolism, phenomenology structures itself by
employing a notion of the Ideal. One of the important arguments
that Edmund Husserl made at the beginning of the twentieth
century was that the qualia with which phenomenology
concerned itself were acts of consciousness. That is to say, the
world as it appears to us and as it presents itself to our mind is
entirely fashioned in and through our consciousness. For this
reason, the object of study for phenomenology has always been
that which we have claimed to be conscious of – the objects we
see and the events that we witness happen around us, other
people, even ourselves in certain circumstances. Understood in
this way, our interaction with the world is a purely cerebral one,
or as Husserl put it, one of "intention." We navigate the world by
considering all the sense-data that we collect as we walk, say,
along a city street.

The fact that Martin Heidegger took issue with Husserl's
intentional account of phenomenology explains Harman's
attraction to the writing of the German philosopher. In
collapsing the formative role that Husserl gave to intention (or
what we might understand casually here as cognition),
Heidegger, intentionally or not (forgive the pun!), loosened the
grip that the Ideal exerted over our experience of the world.
What Heidegger managed to do in his hugely influential book
Being and Time (1927) was to demonstrate that the vast majority

of our encounters with the world happen subconsciously or, put another way, "other to" our thinking mind. In order to demonstrate his point, Heidegger turned to our use of tools. Take the humble hammer. For Heidegger, when we use a hammer to complete a building project of some kind, we do not continue to think of the hammer in our hand as an object independent from ourselves. Put simply, while we happily hammer away at a nail on a piece of wood, we have no conscious recognition of the hammer. In fact, we have no conscious recognition of the hammer, the nails, or the work-bench. These objects that we *could* think about and theorize about if we wished, *become phenomenologically transparent* when being used.

It is a startling claim, and one that we are perhaps resistant to on first reading. But let me put it another way – I think I can give another example of objects becoming phenomenologically transparent that is harder hitting than Heidegger's hammer! Consider... the air that you are breathing right now. Right up until I asked you to think about it, I suspect that, as the saying goes, "you hadn't given it a second thought." But nonetheless, while you have been reading this book you have up until this point been inhaling and exhaling air, expanding and compressing your lungs, and oxygenating your blood without ever being conscious of it. This is exactly what Heidegger is saying about tool-use. Until we actually consider the object in itself, the object that we are "using" is to all intents and purposes indistinguishable from ourselves. In fact, we become so absorbed in the activities that we undertake (building a wardrobe, breathing, and so on) that we also begin to lose an awareness of ourselves (how is your big toe right now?). Phenomenologically speaking, Heidegger showed that what we think of as subjects and objects actually disappear in the moment of ongoing activity.

Of course, everything changes when the hammer breaks or the quality of the air decreases (or our mouth becomes covered, and so on). When the hammer breaks we become again a subject and the hammer becomes an object of contemplation. Unable to do its job, we consider again the object in our hand ensuring that it is no longer phenomenologically transparent. In fact, the hammer becomes conspicuous in our hand, and we search intellectually for ways to overcome the interruption to our previous activity. That is to say, we think again about the object, about its uses and how it functions, about its qualities and dimensions. This is where we re-encounter Husserl's intentional objects; in the realm of broken tools.

For many critics, this is Heidegger explaining that praxis precedes theory – that our use of things comes before our theorization of things. But for Harman, there is something else that one must take away from this tool-analysis. Rather than a discussion of praxis over theory or a recognition of the tacit practical context in which all theory is grounded, Harman uses Heidegger's tool-analysis as further evidence that the practical use of an object tells us no more about the essential quality of the object than does our theorization of it. No matter whether it is used or broken, Heidegger's hammer exhibits an essential, but nonetheless inscrutable and inexhaustible, reality that lies somewhere beyond "the accessible theoretical, practical, or perceptual qualities of the hammer" (Harman 2012, 187).

And there is more. From Heidegger's observation that none of this relies on a subject that is cognizant of the qualities of the objects that it uses, Harman concludes that all objects must encounter each other in exactly this same way. "Raindrops or breezes that strike the hammer may not be 'conscious' of it in human fashion," he writes, "yet such entities fail to exhaust the reality of the hammer to no less a degree than human praxis or theory" (2012, 187). Given that the essential reality of all objects "withdraws" from every kind of encounter in this way, regardless of whether those encounters are with objects of the animate or inanimate world, we must conclude that the human encounter with the world is not as unique as philosophers such as Kant maintained. Again, it is worth paying attention to Harman:

> The withdrawal of objects is not some cognitive trauma that afflicts only humans and a few smart animals, but expresses the permanent inadequacy of any relation at all. If there is no way to make a hammer perfectly present to my thought or action, there is also no way to make cotton present to fire, or glass to raindrops. (2011a, 40)

In short, everything "withdraws" from everything else, and because of this we necessarily lose the privileged relationship with the world that Kant granted us. Put like this, Harman makes Heidegger's work question Kant in a way that Heidegger never did. While for Kant the noumenal world merely haunts human awareness with a specter of its own limited capacity to know the world (something we could call "human finitude"), for Harman the human/world coupling has no higher status than any other coupling. Following in the vein of Alfred North Whitehead, Harman concludes,

> All relations are on exactly the same footing. This does not entail a projection of human properties onto the non-human world, but rather the reverse: what it says is that the crude prehensions made by minerals and dirt are no less relations than are the sophisticated mental activity of humans. Instead of placing souls into sand and stones, we find something sandy or stony in the human soul. (2011a, 42)

So ends the reign of Man and the Ideal, for the kind of realism outlined here simply cannot support such a hierarchy. Understood like this, the world is composed of real objects that ultimately resist "all forms of causal or cognitive mastery" (Harman 2012, 188).

Again, then, speculative realism shares some of the basic observations about the world made by the Symbolist poets – that the world is cleaved in two, and one of those sides is inaccessible to human interrogation. But at the same time it strongly resists the conclusions that the Symbolists drew from this observation. In short, the faith that the Symbolist poets invested in the Ideal has always been one step too far for the speculative realist. In his preface to René Ghil's *Treatise on the Word* (1886), Mallarmé said that his aim was to perceive, beyond a real flower, the ideal flower that can never be found in this world:

> I say: a flower! and, out of the oblivion into which my voice consigns any real shape, as something other than petals known to man, there rises, harmoniously and gently, the ideal flower itself, the one that is absent from all earthly bouquets. (Ghil 1886, 6)

And from this Mallarmé drew the conclusion that the point of poetry itself is to create ideal forms, "the pure concept, unlinked to any related or material form" (Ghil 1886, 6). What this demonstrates perfectly well is that for the Symbolists the value of any object in the world lies solely in its capacity or ability to reveal the absolute. Understood like this, everything in the world around us is to be regarded as nothing more than a marker, or at best a sign, of a transcendent realm that we will never be able to touch.

But the core contention of speculative realism is that one must rediscover again the material world around us. As such, to invoke the Ideal is to organize a transcendental plane – a reality that exists above the material world that we encounter – that ultimately swallows the objects of the world whole. This is the mistake of the great French Symbolist poets. For those who follow object-oriented thought, the objects of the material world are all that are needed in order to be able to talk about its functioning. To this extent, speculative realism holds a rugged materialist disposition – that the world is composed of objects, and that these objects interact and organize themselves in a way that is capable of describing every observation that we can make of it. There is then no compulsion to add an extra-material "something" in speculative-realist thought as a means to lend an air of a pleasing unity to our world and in so doing explain the emergence of objects (such as "God," for example, or Baruch Spinoza's "immanent, singular substance"). As Harman writes, there are just "real individual objects" that fail to exhaust the reality of other "real individual objects" (2012, 188). The question is, as Baudelaire and Mallarmé well-knew, how to write of such objects.

3

Literary Theory and the Impulse to Mine

So, French Symbolism gives us the correct question to ask of the world but, according to those interested in object-oriented philosophy at least, leaves behind a deeply unsatisfactory answer for us to consider. For the speculative realist, recourse to the Ideal privileges the human encounter with the world in a way that cannot be justified. Indeed, Graham Harman has been at pains to insist that the human/world relationship cannot be thought of as somehow superior to or more important than any other object/world relationship. The world may be split between the noumenal and the phenomenal, but the distance this schism imposes between the world and our capacity to know it is in no way unique to the human condition. Again, then, fire does not exhaust the cotton it burns, nor rain the ground upon which it lands, nor the human the stone she examines in her hand.

For this reason, we should certainly think of speculative realism as something that sits comfortably within what Richard Grusin has identified as "the nonhuman turn" in the contemporary humanities.[8] This turn, properly understood, is not an attempt to remove the human from the world, but rather an attempt to resituate us through a less (or, preferably non-) androcentric understanding of things. Whether or not one thinks of the nonhuman in terms of the animal, discussions about affectivity, materiality, technology, or our proper role in organic and geophysical systems, it is clear that the human encounter with the world in whichever guise it has assumed has only ever been one species of encounter within a sea of encounters. As Timothy Morton explains:

I *anthropomorphize*. It's not that I anthropomorphize in some situations and not in others. It's that, because of the fact of phenomenological *sincerity*, I can't help anthropomorphizing everything I handle [...] It is impossible for me to peel myself away from the totality of my phenomenological being. [But] just as I fail to avoid anthropomorphizing everything, so all entities [...] constantly translate other objects into their own terms. (Morton 2012, 207)

Here, Morton makes clear that just as we *must* translate our engagement with the world in a very particular way, so too must every other object or entity of the world. In other words, everything encounters the world in its own unique way. That is to say, a dog encounters the world in a specifically dog-like way (we can only imagine how a dog's sense of smell organizes a perception of the environment that is radically different to that of the human), just as a tree must encounter the world in a specifically tree-like way, and the wind must encounter the world in an explicitly wind-like way.[9]

But beyond this relativization of the human experience of the world, the nonhuman turn also shows how the human can (and must) be thought in nonhuman ways. There are few better examples of this than that offered by the achingly contemporary phrase, "the Anthropocene." The Anthropocene refers to a period of geological time that recognizes the profound impact that the human has had within and on the Earth's climate and geology. Some trace this impact back to 10,000 BC and the birth of agriculture, while others look no further than the Trinity Test of 1945 that ushered in the Nuclear Age. Most though, stick the pin in the chart of human history somewhere towards the end of the eighteenth century – the first years that the carbon produced by the coal-fired industry of Britain began to be deposited worldwide. However, regardless of where one looks to actually settle in this debate, what is important to note is that each date talks to a moment when the human became a profoundly influential agent within and on the Earth's climate and geology. Or put another way, each date talks to a moment when the human became a climatological or geological force on the planet – "a climatological or geological force" that, as Grusin observes, "operates just as a nonhuman would, independent of human will, belief, or desires" (2015, vii).

Although seemingly posting the human front and center in a consideration of the world, a proper interrogation of the Anthropocene therefore means thinking "the human" purely through its nonhuman agency. This is not only because the individual human is lost to the mass of humanity-in-itself, but because what is important about the human here is a pre-individualized, depersonalized (or rather a-personalized) capacity to act. In other words, the Anthropocene is about the weight of humanity acting in spite of the actions of the individual, and as we shall see in the next chapter, that has everything to do with recognizing the fact that the object-in-itself is much more than the sum of its parts.

However, what is important for us to understand here is that this kind of relativization of the human in association with an ability to conceptualize it in terms that are strictly non-human (that is, for example, as a force of nature) necessitates the same kind of revisionary assessment of the form and function of literature and literary criticism that was demanded by its forerunners in the nonhuman turn – that is, those disciplines such as ecocriticism, animal studies, and the work conducted on the posthuman(ities). It is then this revision to the art and architecture of literary criticism that I want to pursue over the following few chapters. I ask myself amongst other things: what are the consequences of thinking about literature in this particular context? How are we to think of the event of literature if it is to be understood as a nonhuman phenomenon? What does the literary text look like if we understand it as an object in and of itself? In order to ask these kinds of questions of literature we have of course to travel (admittedly at pace) through a few schools of literary criticism that have left their influence on the way in which the contemporary critic thinks about literature. But, in seeing the kind of revisions demanded by this account of things, we will begin to discern the shape and character of a literary criticism that is inflected with the concerns of object-oriented philosophy.

There have been many ways of understanding the literary text, as those who have read such luminaries as Plato, Aristotle, Longinus, Sidney, Dryden, Pope, Burke, Coleridge, and Arnold can attest. But I think it is fair to say that the most sustained engagement with the question of literature proper occurred in the twentieth century. Indeed, the 1960s and 1970s marked a great explosion in the theory of literature, as the children of WWII reacted against the formalist paradigm of their fathers who had continued to valorize the literary text as a product of a lone genius who could not only intuit but also represent the universal truths of human life. It is interesting to us, though, that those revolutionary scholars of the mid-twentieth century who set about reimagining the event of literature did so in a remarkably orthodox way. As Graham Harman has noted, just like the contemporary philosopher, the contemporary literary theorist has by and large been committed to "mining" literary works in order to reveal or formulate a more profound account of their being. That is to say, literary theorists have actively been engaged in doing away with thinking about the literary work as an object in its own right. In an attempt to know it better, theorists have either delved into the literary work in order to grasp its constitutive features or they have sought to contextualize it. While of course both strategies aim to deepen our understanding of the text in hand (and they certainly do), it is clear that they do so at the expense of understanding the literary work as an object-in-itself. This is an important point for Harman and central to his object-oriented philosophy – *any theory of literature or literary criticism that is inflected with the concerns of object-oriented philosophy must refocus critical attention back towards the literary work as an object-in-itself.*

In light of the significance of the point being made here, it is perhaps sensible to spend a little time making clear exactly what Harman means when he talks of the mining of objects (literary or otherwise). And to this end, it is perhaps wise to begin by making clear that such mining can take on more than one form. The first species of mining that Harman discusses is perhaps the most common, for it is the way that most of us have been trained to think about objects in the world. Harman calls it *undermining*. Undermining refers to the act of drilling down into the interior of an object with the intention of revealing its genetic, constitutive, or fundamental elements. To do so, it is supposed, a more profound version of reality is revealed. For example, tables are not (just) those things upon which we place things; they are in fact a collection of atoms that have attained a certain configuration from expressing a certain energetic state. In terms of the literary world, undermining describes precisely the style of approach that structuralism took to the literary text. Indeed, the structuralist enterprise has often been characterized as the act of breaking the surface of the text in order to reveal the deeper qualities that lie beneath.

Speaking broadly, structuralism perceives the literary work as the manifestation of a complex subterranean system that underlies all human social and cultural practice. As such, it is only interested in grasping (or elucidating) what it thinks of as the universal structure that codes a particular text. In other words, structuralism is only interested in the specifics of a literary text to the extent that it can be used to demonstrate the operation of a wider or more profound structure working away below the surface. Since this underground mechanism is a feature of the text, structuralism adopts something of an anti-humanistic mien

– thinking of itself as sitting in "opposition to all forms of literary criticism in which the human subject is the source and origin of literary meaning" (Selden et al 2005, 62). That is to say, as far as the structuralist is concerned, the text holds the key to its own meaning. But again, in order to get at that meaning of the literary text, structuralism holds that one must at the very least break the surface of the text – the text must be excavated.

It is an approach to literature that ultimately emerges from the hugely influential work of the Swiss linguist, Ferdinand de Saussure. At the beginning of the twentieth century, Saussure postulated that the language that we speak is the product of a fundamental gap between word and world. For Saussure, the words that we speak are "signs" – which is to say, composite forms made up of a "signifier" (the written or spoken mark) and a "signified" (the thought or image of what is said or written). Understood like this, our language is best thought of as a sign-system – that is to say, language is the system by which signs (or as we would usually say, words) develop a meaning. The common example that is given to elucidate this thesis asks us to consider the humble traffic light. Imagine we approach a set of traffic lights, and the light visible is red. This is our "sign" – the lit red traffic light. Now, the lit red traffic light does not just say to us, "Look! A lit red light." Rather, it acts as a signifier, which is to say it tells us something more than just what color it is. It says to us, "Stop!" All well and good, then. But it is important to recognize that we only develop this specific reaction to red traffic lights – the impulse to stop, in this case – because it has a place within a sign-system. That is to say, it is because it is part of the traffic-light signaling system that we know red, in this instance, means "stop."

If our language only had three terms to its name then it would work in exactly the same way as a set of traffic lights. But of course, our languages are much more complicated than this – certain languages, it has been estimated, containing close to one-million individual terms. There are some grand extrapolations to draw from this, but the one in which we are interested concerns what Saussure's model tells us about the nature of our spoken languages. If we agree with Saussure that our language is a sign-system, then it must be true that our language is something that floats above the surface of the world, never making earthly contact with it. Indeed, Saussure's model of language shows that meaning (what a sign means) is a product of language itself (the specific sign-system) rather than a product of language actually "touching" or representing the world as it is. That is to say, there is nothing essential about the word "tree" that connects it to the thing that sticks out of the ground. The significance of this observation is that "instead of saying that an author's language reflects reality, the structuralists argue that the structure of language produces 'reality'" (Selden et al 2005, 78). In other words, meaning cannot be regarded as something that is determined by the individual; meaning is something that can only emerge from the system. In terms of the study of literature, that "system" is the subterranean structure that makes possible the meaning of the literary work. And understood like this, the job of the structuralist critic is to identify the structure(s) that allow a literary text to "mean."

The Russian folklorist Vladimir Propp was certainly one of the first to make good on this search for the hidden structures that scaffold narrative. In chapter three of his seminal book *Morphology of the Folktale* (1958), Propp outlines thirty-one units of narrative, or "functions," which describe the significant actions that form the folktale narrative. It is this "series of functions," Propp writes, that "represents the morphological foundation of fairy tales in general" (1958, 23). According to Propp then, the first five functions of a fairy tale are:

1. One of the members of a family absents himself from home
2. An interdiction is addressed to the hero

3. The interdiction is violated
4. The villain makes an attempt at reconnaissance
5. The villain receives information about his victim

And, as one might expect, Propp goes on to explain the various ways in which each one of these functions is composed in different fairy tales. So, for the eighth function of the common fairy tale – "The villain causes harm or injury to a member of a family" – Propp offers a list of nineteen different ways in which this function is expressed in the literature. The first five are:

1. The villain abducts a person
2. The villain seizes or takes away a magical agent
3. The villain pillages or spoils the crops
4. The villain seizes the daylight
5. The villain plunders in other forms

The way in which Propp thinks of the fairy tale is therefore as a series of more or less interchangeable narrative elements. By Propp's own reckoning, the author simply chooses and arranges already-functioning elements from a well-established reservoir of such elements.

The charge for those who followed Propp in this vein of criticism was to research in other genres of literature in order to determine whether or not a "universal grammar" could be found that underscored all literature. While this challenge was taken up by such important writers as A. J. Greimas, Tzvetan Todorov, and Gérard Genette, it is to the voice of the important literary theorist Jonathan Culler that we should pay attention, for he makes a key observation about this programmatic method of structuralism for us. Reminding himself of Roland Barthes's observation in *Critique et vérité* (1966), Culler writes that structuralist "poetics bears […] not so much on the work itself as on its intelligibility" (2004, 143). Put another way, the object-text disappears in order to make way for something more fundamental – the structure that grants "intelligibility." Similarly, the influential literary theorist and critic Raman Selden concludes:

the structuralist neglects the specificity of actual texts, and treats them as if they were like the patterns of iron filings produced by an invisible force [...] Not only the text but also the author is cancelled as the structuralist places in brackets the actual work and the person who wrote it, in order to isolate the true object of enquiry – the system. (Selden et al 2005, 77)

So, the structuralist theorist ignores the literary work as an object in its own right by diving down into the mechanics of the narrative in order to divine a more profound account of its being.

But this act of undermining is only one way in which the literary theorist or philosopher can mine an object. In addition to the act of undermining that looks to drill down into an object in order to grasp a more profound understanding of its ontological condition, Harman has identified the act of *over-mining* – a critique that moves upwards and away from the object under discussion. That is to say, over-mining concerns those critiques that look to discern the significance of an object merely by locating it within a chain of external relations. Since we have already discussed structuralism, it might be best to use poststructuralism as our example here.

In many ways, poststructuralism can be thought of as a reactionary concern with the issues brought to light by structuralism. And if we are to caricature it like this, by far my favorite way of doing so is given by Raman Selden: "poststructuralists are structuralists who suddenly see the error of their ways" (Selden et al 2005, 144). The error to which Selden refers here concerns the structuralist treatment of language. Whereas structuralism posited a "universal grammar" for language – that

is, a system that allowed for the very possibility of language itself
– poststructuralism looked to theorize the way in which language
was actually used by the individual. In so doing, it abandoned all
claims to the objectivity of both language and the study of
language, and instead turned towards the "speaking subject." In
other words, poststructuralism looked to privilege the way in
which the individual actually used language. The most dramatic
consequence of this turn to the concern of the subjective
processes by which one talks was the realization that structures
and systems are second-order phenomena. Put another way,
contra structuralism, poststructuralism posits that "chaos"
(eventually) assumes (some kind of) order.

Jacques Derrida, who is perhaps the most-widely known
poststructuralist thinker, made the point clear in a hugely influential lecture that he presented at Johns Hopkins University in
1966. In this lecture, titled "Structure, Sign, and Play in the
Discourse of the Human Sciences," Derrida critiqued the idea of
the center. He argued that the center that people always look to
as a means to orient their being – God, consciousness, Truth, and
so on – is in fact a bundle of qualities that are in constant tension
with each other. As such, these "centers" only continue to work
for us as modes of orientation if we do not examine their constitution too deeply. Any such interrogation, Derrida argued, would
quickly reveal not only the fabricated nature of such core ideas as
these, but also the chaos of relations in tension that constantly
churn away underneath the seeming coherence of the sign.

Derrida's point here is that although our language appears to
be coherent, the words upon which it rests mask a great chaos of
meaning. No sign is unified; no word (especially in isolation)
means anything. Indeed, the fact that words cannot be traced
back to the phenomenal world, that they lack a core essence upon
which we can rely, makes clear that language cannot get us to the
point where we can claim an objective or essential meaning for
anything. Meaning, as Derrida sees it, is endlessly deferred.

Think here of how we turn to a dictionary in order to try and understand the meaning of an unfamiliar word only to discover that our unfamiliar word is "elucidated" by other words, and those words are in turn elucidated by yet more words, and so on *ad infinitum*. For the poststructuralist, meaning is therefore the point at which the subject looks to bring to an end what can only be understood as the endless play of associations that contour a sign. Put simply, meaning is always a profoundly subjective and provisional moment of interruption.

It is then precisely this kind of chain of signification that must be interrupted in order to produce meaning, this endless relationality of words, the infinite way in which we can contextualize any object, which Harman has in mind when he talks about the act of over-mining. In this moment, the object of enquiry is exploded upwards – which is to say, lost to the network of infinite relations in which it sits. We know the meaning of a word not because we can reach its core essence, but rather because it is not *this* word, or *that* word, or any other word.

In poststructuralist thought, this negative ontology (that is, a way of thinking about the being of objects in the world by putting them into a chain of relations and then deciding what it *is not*) is not only true for the word but also for the book to which such words give birth. For example, the important Bulgarian-French philosopher Julia Kristeva and others have shown the way in which the larger object of the literary work is only meaningful as something that takes part in a wider circuit of literature. For Kristeva, literature is born in the weave of textual relations. "Any text," she writes, "is constructed of a mosaic of quotations; any text is the absorption and transformation of another" (1986, 37). That is to say, no text emerges simply from the ether; no text can stand alone. Rather, each individual literary work is the product of an infinitely rich, infinitely complex set of relations with other literary works. It is for this reason, then, that poststructuralism has learned to think of every literary work as an *event* rather than an *object* – that is, as something that happens through or with time, rather than that which supposedly happens in spite of time.

So, undermining tears objects asunder by looking for a deeper reality within the object itself while over-mining ignores the object in hand by looking for a deeper reality described by the chains of association in which the object sits. It is almost written in the stars then that Harman's third species of mining will also in some way abandon the object-in-itself. And of course, it does. Harman's third species of analytical mining is called *duo-mining*, and given our previous discussions of the mining techniques of structuralism and poststructuralism, we should already be amply aware of it. Why? Because duo-mining responds to that sense of awkwardness one encounters when trying to characterize an analytical movement. That is to say, it responds to the sense we have that both undermining and over-mining can take place at the same time. For example, the way in which structuralism undermines a literary text in search of its fundamental structures inevitably leads to an over-mined way of thinking about literature proper – that is, as an undifferentiated "multidimensional space," Roland Barthes would say, which only takes shape from the way in which the writer redistributes or reassembles the chain of associations that constitute the "always already written" (Barthes 1977, 143). Similarly, poststructuralism's over-mining of the literary text is the result of the sustained undermining of the text – the attempt to drive a wedge between the signifier and the signified and in so doing unsettle the coherence of the sign.

Understood like this, mining is clearly a more complicated business than we might have first thought. But nonetheless, if we are to attempt to think the literary text as an object-in-itself, we must resist the analytical impulse towards undermining, over-mining, or duo-mining the literary work. Indeed, treated as a Harmanian object, the literary theorist and critic is obliged to think of the literary text as an object-in-itself. That is to say, she must think of the text itself as the most profound level of reality. For this critic, there is nothing to be gained from going above or the below the text. It is simply with the text itself that the object-oriented literary critic must concern herself.

Interestingly, this is not the first time that "the text itself" has been the predominant concern for the literary critic. Indeed, this very phrase was the slogan under which a group of scholars united in an attempt to write a new style of literary criticism. This New Criticism, as it came to be known, was a formalist reaction against a biographical-historical criticism that had dominated the study of literature into the early decades of the twentieth century. Under-theorized, literary criticism in the West before the 1930s was simply the task of trying to reveal what the author had intended the reader to understand about the text. In trying to answer this question, critics typically turned to the letters, diaries, and essays of authors as well as biographical and historical material, and in so doing constantly ran the risk of actually failing to examine the text in hand. Ultimately, as Lois Tyson writes, these early "scholars viewed the literary text merely as an adjunct to history, as an illustration of the 'spirit of the age' in which it was written, not as an art object worthy of study in its own right" (2006, 136). And, it is this that the New Critics looked to correct.

New Criticism emerged in the late 1930s as a means to resituate the concern of literature with the text itself. As such, chief amongst its aims was the severance of the literary text (which it regarded with the same pious reverence as that of earlier generations) from the extra-textual material that inevitably developed and surrounded it. As Selden writes,

New Criticism is clearly characterized in premise and practice: it is not concerned with *context* – historical, biographical, intellectual and so on; it is not interested in "fallacies" of "intention" or "affect"; it is concerned solely with the "text in itself," with its language and organization. (Selden et al 2005, 19)

Indeed, New Criticism was openly hostile to maneuvers which aimed to contextualize the text at hand, promoting instead the "objective," "scientific" study of the words as they appeared on the page. The well-known and influential essay penned by William Wimsatt and Monroe Beardsley, "The Intentional Fallacy" (1946), makes the point clear. Here they argue that nothing "outside of the poem" should exert authority over it – including the poet (1946, 471). Understood like this, the poem should be regarded as an object-in-itself. "The poem is not the critic's own," Wimsatt and Beardsley write, "and not the author's (it is detached from the author at birth and goes about the world beyond his power to intend about it or control it)" (1946, 470). And as such, it must stand or fall on whether it works as a poem.

This idea of thinking about the way a poem "works" gives birth to what is surely one of the most memorable lines from serious literary criticism. Wimsatt and Beardsley exclaim, "Judging a poem is like judging a pudding or a machine. One demands that it work" (1946, 469). That is to say, the proof of the pudding is in the eating! It matters not what one imagines the intention to be that lies behind a poem; it only matters that the poem itself works "by the art of the poem itself" (Wimsatt and Beardsley 1946, 469). And this tells us all we need to know about how the New Critics conceived of the literary text – as a *"timeless, autonomous (self-sufficient) object"* (Tyson 2006, 137); as a literary machine that pre-exists the act of interpretation, for meaning was clearly locked into the very fabric of the text.

Understood as a text/machine, the only approach that the literary critic could take to the poem was to try and understand what allowed it to function. That is to say, the New Critics saw as their job the need to reveal the internal coherency of a text – that which allowed it to "speak." So it was that they paid special attention to the formal elements of a text (its images, symbols, metaphors, rhyme, meter, point of view, and so on) and how those elements worked together (whether they were in "creative tension" or a "pleasing sympathy" with each other) in order to produce a stable meaning of the literary work. According to this formulation then, the art of literary criticism was to be thought of as more in keeping with science than anything else – the critic, a man who was to be conscious of adopting a cold air of impersonality so that he might reveal the single best interpretation of the supposedly objective meaning that was locked into the fabric of each literary work.

We can get a clear sense of this by looking over the pages of *The Well-Wrought Urn* (1947), a hugely influential book on literary criticism written by perhaps the leading New Critic of his day, Cleanth Brooks. He writes, for example, that a poem is "a structure of meanings, evaluations, and interpretations; and the principle of unity which informs it seems to be one of balancing and harmonizing connotations, attitudes, and meanings" (1947, 195). Actually, for Brooks this describes all literature, not just poetry. And for this reason, the question of whether a piece of writing is good or not can be answered somewhat objectively. According to critics like Brooks, what makes for truly great literature is when the formal elements of a text come together in perfect sympathy with each other. Just listen to the way in which he describes the structure of the ideal poem:

> The structure of a poem resembles that of a ballet or musical composition. It is a pattern of resolutions and balances and harmonizations, developed through a temporal scheme. (1947, 203)

Here, every textual element finds its correct place and because of that functions in perfect sympathy with every other element.

The ideal poem is therefore a perfectly choreographed ballet, and one that reveals the New Critic's obsession with the condition of "the relation of each item to the whole context" (Brooks 1947, 207).

Of course, what Brooks is actually describing when he talks of the ideal poem in this way is a perfectly functioning machine – a machine whose parts (that is, the formal elements of a text) unambiguously move towards the same meaning, and in so doing create the image of a perfectly coherent textual unity. But this rendition of the literary text as a machine that can be described and understood through the way in which its formal elements mesh together shows well why an object-oriented inflected criticism must move beyond the concerns of New Criticism. We have already seen the skepticism that object-oriented philosophy has for chasing relations as a means of trying to know better an object at hand. Not only does rabid contextualization ultimately result in the loss of the object-in-itself, but the relations that we must look to in order to understand better our object of interest necessarily "translate or distort that to which they relate" (Harman 2011a, 40). Every encounter distorts the object of enquiry. Moreover, as Harman makes clear, "objects must be an excess or surplus outside their current range of relations" (2012, 191) or else they must be forever static, unable to change or evolve. And we know that not to be true. What this means is that as far as object-oriented philosophy is concerned, relations can never exhaust the object to which they relate – *the object will always be this or that set of relations and more.*

Why is this important to our discussion of New Criticism? Well, because although New Criticism turned towards the "text itself" in an effort to maintain the literary work as an object in its own right, it did so not by severing the relations by which earlier generations had made sense of texts, but by simply folding those relations into the literary text itself. That is to say, whereas the romantic-humanist critic saw value in examining the relationship between the literary text and its historical and biographical points of production, New Criticism turned this examination of external relations inward in order to concentrate on the relationship between the formal elements of the text. For this reason, the object-oriented critic must distance herself from New Criticism for exactly the same reasons that the New Critic distanced himself from the criticism of earlier generations. While the New Critic would claim that the formal examination of a text's interior offers a richer interpretation of a literary text to that pursued through the examination of a text's external relations, the object-oriented critic must insist that the study of internal relations must be subject to exactly the same kind of distortions and acts of translation that are encountered in the study of external relations. In other words, for the object-oriented literary critic, the New Critic's turn to the interiority of the literary text can only result in the same failure of previous generations to fully grasp the text itself.

To this extent, it could be argued that the object-oriented critic takes the New Critic's concern with the act of paraphrase more seriously than the New Critic himself. In what is surely the most widely cited chapter in *The Well-Wrought Urn*, Brooks talks of "the heresy of paraphrase" (chapter 11). Here, Brooks maintains that one cannot hope to reach the meaning of a poem (or any other literary text for that matter) by looking to simply explain it, for this act of translation – that is, of explaining meaning – opens up a gap between word and world (in this instance, a gap between the capacity of language to represent and the poem as it is on the page) in such a way that the text can never be fully apprehended. Therefore, for Brooks and the other New Critics, the poem itself *is* meaning. That is to say, the form and content of the work as it appears on the page are inseparable aspects of each other. "The relationship," Brooks writes, "is not that of an idea 'wrapped in emotion' or a 'prose-sense decorated by sensuous imagery'." No. The relationship is far more "intimate" than this

(1947, 204). Form and content constitute the fabric from which the reader "abstracts" every proposition, idea, or meaning. As such, no proposition, idea, or meaning can ever claim full fidelity with the text from which it is abstracted, and in turn, that means that every proposition, idea, or meaning must stand on its own terms.

Because of this, Brooks suggests that the task of the literary critic must lie away from revealing the meaning of a literary text. Rather the task of the critic is to articulate the mechanisms by which a text coheres and thereby produces (some kind of) meaning. But for the critic who concerns herself with object-oriented thought, the very same relations that the New Critic looks to in order to understand how a text "speaks for itself" must also respect Brooks's law of paraphrase. That is to say, the object-oriented critic sees paraphrase at work in the internal relations of a literary text just as much as the New Critic sees it working outside of the text. As such, although a critic may discern some importance in the employ of, say, ambiguity, paradox, and irony in a text, for the object-oriented literary critic each of these literary devices must only be understood as the paraphrase of a particular machinic operation. In this way, the act of translation that Brooks points towards as a way of saying that the meaning of a poem can only be found in the poem itself, is here seen at play in the internal relations of the text-object. And when the interiority of the literary text is itself understood in terms of (the inadequacy of) paraphrase, then it is surely true that the text-object must be thought of as withdrawing from itself in exactly the same way that every other object withdraws from itself.

It is, then, the ability to see paraphrase everywhere in the world of the text that signals the important extension that the object-oriented literary critic brings to New Critical thought. As the New Critic laments the act of paraphrase in the literary world while at the same time lauding a scientific discourse that seemingly resists such acts of distortion – Brooks once wrote: "a scientific proposition can stand alone. If it is true, it is true" (1947, 207) – then the object-oriented literary critic refuses to cleave the world in this way. Since paraphrase is the natural condition of every encounter, the object-oriented literary critic sees both the literary text and the scientific proposition in exactly the same way – that is, as an attempt to express our encounters with the world. In other words, the gaps which open up between the word and world as a consequence of the failure of paraphrase to fully grasp that which it announces, characterizes *every* aspect of the human encounter with the world. The point to be made then is simple: "the failure of paraphrase is not monopolized by the arts, but haunts all human dealings with the world" (Harman 2012, 190). As such, whether it is through a standard language, the language of mathematics, or any other form of human translation, "any attempt to translate this reality into masterable knowledge for logocentric purposes will fail" (Harman 2012, 196). Not just because being is deeper than every logos, but because as humans we can only work in the key of paraphrase.

4

The Text as a (Failing) Machine

Nonetheless, the idea of the literary text as a machine is something that is worth pursuing here, for this formulation of the text ultimately responds in the best way to the demands of the nonhuman turn in which speculative realism takes place. Indeed, once one begins to think of the literary text as a machine then it becomes easier to regard it in the same way that speculative realism insists all objects should be regarded – that is, as an object-in-itself. What I want to do in this chapter then, is outline the character of the literary text as it emerges from this new respect for the object-in-itself. Certainly, it is a characterization that inherits elements from the school of New Criticism. After all, it shares the New Critic's concern for the "text itself" and thereby the willingness to be done with the idea of a presiding author who maintains the key to a literary work that must be thought of as a book of secrets to be unlocked. That is to say, this character-ization of the literary text shares the anti-humanist drive of New Criticism. But at the same time, it differs from the teachings of New Criticism in a number of significant ways. It is the character of these "significant differences" with which this chapter is concerned.

I want to begin, then, by turning to Levi Bryant's important work *Onto-Cartography* (2014). In this book, which Bryant describes as a defense of a materialism that has been severely eroded by the intellectual obsession with discursivity in twentieth-century thought, Bryant attempts to show the ways in which objects exhibit a power to act. Realizing that "the signifier, meaning, belief, and so on are not the sole agencies structuring social relations" (2014, 3), Bryant posits a world full of "stuff" – that is, material objects such as "trees, rocks, planets, stars" (2014,

6) – that makes itself felt on and in the human world regardless of whether or not we are cognizant of it. And to this extent, the book can be thought of as something that simply rehearses the basic tenets of speculative realism. That is until about half way through the introduction to the book when things begin to change dramatically. After describing a world constituted of "individual entities existing at a variety of different levels of scale," Bryant states, "I call these entities machines" (2014, 6). It is this rewriting and rethinking of the "object" as "machine" that changes everything. This turn to the machine marks a turn to a machine-oriented ontology (rather than an object-oriented ontology), and the result is the opening up of profound new avenues of engagement for the philosopher and the literary critic alike.

First, this turn to the machine emphasizes what Bryant sees as "the manner in which entities dynamically *operate* on inputs producing outputs" (2014, 6). In other words, Bryant's picture of a world composed entirely of machines means that we can no longer be overly-concerned with what something *is* (that is, explorations of ontology). Rather the concern of the philosopher and the critic is necessarily directed towards the product(s) of such machines – with what machines can *do*. To be clear, this is a concern that does not emerge from the analysis of *how* a machine functions (which as we saw in the previous chapter was the concern of New Criticism); it is an interest that arises from a direct analysis of the operation(s) of a particular machine – which is to say, the transformation of inputs that flow through machines and the variety of different types of outputs that they produce.

Second, such a machine-oriented ontology does away with over 400 years of intellectual enquiry dominated by the subject/object relationship. In Bryant's model, the world is not the product of human invention, nor is it the result of the imposition of the external world on the psychic landscape of the human.

Rather, the world is the product of the ways in which innumerable and diverse machines ceaselessly encounter each other. Here, the figure of the human is necessarily embedded in a broader natural world – the result of a specific arrangement and engagement of particular machines. Relativizing the position of the human in this way, Bryant's machine-oriented ontology reconfigures the (human) subject / (nonhuman) object relationship as a flat ontology – which is to say, a record of being that finally dispenses with hierarchies. In other words, unlike the vertical organization of humanism, here there are no "higher" or "lower" functioning machines, there are no dominating or "grand" machines, *there are only machines that function in this way or that way.*

And it is this observation that leads on to the third revisionary aspect that Bryant's machine-oriented account of the world brings to the stable of speculative-realist thought. In a world composed entirely of machines, our critical interest must shift away from the kind of discussion of aesthetics that dominates the object-oriented philosophy of such influential writers as Graham Harman and Timothy Morton. Why? Because we cannot be as interested in the way in which appearance and essence trip over each other as we are in the products of the encounters between machines. As we shall see, when machines encounter each other they constitute a network that ultimately increases the power of every machine involved in that encounter to act. As such, our critical attention must be drawn to determining the character and dimension of this notion of a machine's "power to act."

However, before we can begin this program of enquiry we must first be clear about what we mean when we speak of machines. And on this matter, I am willing to defer to the work of Bryant. For Bryant, a machine is "the name for any entity, material or immaterial, corporeal or incorporeal, that exists." That is to say, as far as Bryant is concerned, when we use words such as *entity, object, existent, substance, body,* and *thing,* what we are actually talking about are machines. Indeed, all of these words are synonyms of *machine* (Bryant 2014, 15). Understood like this, our entryway into Bryant's machine-oriented ontology is a fairly simple matter – machines are simply the "stuff" that fills the world.

But if we are to accept this definition of a machine, we must at the same time confront and dispel some of the more naturalized assumptions that we carry about the nature of machines. Indeed, we must strike them from our thinking because some of the persistent ideas that we tend to harbor about machines can only compromise a proper understanding of what Bryant means when he talks of a machine-oriented ontology. Let us begin then with what is perhaps the most enduring precon-ception about machines: *all machines are rigid machines*. Certainly, rigid machines exist, and when we are asked to think about a machine it is perhaps true that we think first of a rigid machine – that is, an object composed of fixed but moving parts, like a car, or a lawnmower, or a dishwasher. These are machines that have been designed for a specific purpose, and they carry out this purpose unchangingly until the law of entropy takes over and they finally wear out and breakdown. However, that being said, what defines rigid machines is not so much that they endlessly repeat a function but that they cannot "grow" or "develop" "as a consequence of what they have learned" (Bryant 2014, 16). In other words, rigid machines are destined to endlessly repeat the same function and their only reward for doing so is their eventual demise. Understood like this, and put into a context in which every thing is also a machine, it is clear that such diverse objects as rocks, comets, Styrofoam, and plastics are good examples of rigid machines. But clearly, that does not describe every object in the world. What of plants, people, and penguins? These too are machines in the sense that they make up the stuff of the universe, but it is obvious that they do not belong to the class of rigid machines. Indeed, their very existence proves that the rigid machine is just one class of an entire kingdom of machines.

The next assumption about machines that Bryant confronts in his book is the idea that *all machines are designed*. Again, our common experience of the world would seem to bear this out – cars, lawnmowers, and washing machines are all designed. But since our understanding of the machine stretches to *every object* in the world we have to be careful here. If by "designed" we mean the mapping of the specific functions of a machine by a (human) consciousness, then it is clear that most machines of the world are in fact not designed. For, such a definition would immediately exclude machines like trees, rocks, and planets. Of course, those who follow the baseless doctrine of "intelligent design" might take issue with this point, but the point of fact is that our understanding of evolution and natural selection caters perfectly well to the observations that we have made of *bios*. For instance, there is perhaps no clearer example of historical legacy in the human than the circuitous route taken by the recurrent laryngeal nerve. It is a nerve that runs from the brain down to the chest, where it loops around one of the main arteries only to move back up towards the larynx. Importantly, the distance from the start of the nerve to its end point is commonly in the order of just four or five inches, while the nerve itself is commonly some seven times longer. What accounts for the large disparity between the length (and route) of the nerve and its points of connection is the fact that it is an inheritance from our piscine past. The nerve first developed in fish-like creatures and ran in a very direct fashion from brain to gills (which are close to the heart of fish) to throat. However, once the mammalian neck was introduced into this assemblage it was easier for evolution to continue lengthening the nerve rather than to just "rewire" it, which is surely what an (intelligent) "designer" would have undertaken.[10] What this tells us then is that contrary to the sense we might have of machines as designed objects, the poor "design" of the recurrent laryngeal nerve points to the conclusion that most machines of the world are in fact autopoietic systems – that is to say, most machines of the world are able to reproduce and maintain themselves.

The final assumption that Bryant takes issue with is perhaps the hardest one to shake off, for this assumption maintains that *all machines have a purpose or a use*. It is, I think, an assumption that arises as a natural consequence of the sense we have of all machines as designed objects. If all machines are designed then it seems logical to conclude that all machines must therefore have a purpose or a use. But just like the earlier assumption, this preconception is also wrong. To be sure, some machines do appear to have a purpose – the car, the lawnmower, the tree, the volcano, and so on – but on closer inspection it becomes clear that no machine acts for the sake of anything other than itself. That is to say, neither a tree, nor a rock, nor a planet acts on its own for any other purpose than maintaining itself. Where the confusion lies in this matter is that every machine can be put to a specific use. And of course, this is exactly how ecosystems emerge – one machine benefits from the process of another machine, which in turn benefits from the process of yet another machine, and so on *ad infinitum*. The point to take away, though, is that just because a machine can be put into service, it does not mean that that particular use is an intrinsic feature of the machine. Giving a rather prosaic example, Bryant explains, "Rocks can be used as paperweights, doorstops, weapons when hurled, devices for boiling when heated and placed in water, stones in a wall, and so on. They don't have *a* use, but rather are *put to* a use" (2014, 24).

So, when I talk of machines here I am not necessarily talking about rigid or designed objects that have a supposed purpose. In fact, I am typically talking at odds to this very narrow way of conceiving the notion of the machine because the machine that I am interested in thinking about here is the literary text.

The question "what kind of machine is the literary text?" is certainly an easy one to ask, but the simplicity of the question belies the complexity of the answer. Indeed, it is a question that can only be responded to by negotiating the difference between what Bryant calls "corporeal" and "incorporeal" machines. And surprisingly, the difference between these two phyla is not simply a matter of matter! As Bryant describes it, "a corporeal machine is any machine that is made of matter, that occupies a discrete time and place, and that exists for a duration" (2014, 26). As one might expect, then. However, incorporeal machines are defined not by their immateriality but rather by their "iterability, potential eternity, and the capacity to manifest themselves in a variety of spatial and temporal locations at once while retaining their identity" (Bryant 2014, 26). In other words, incorporeal machines are knowable by the fact that they can repeat themselves endlessly in a multitude of spaces and times simultaneously. What we are talking about here then are things like numbers or theories – that is, things that are not limited to a single instantiation in a particular time and place. And indeed, this is where we find the literary text.

It is tempting to think of the literary text as a simple corporeal machine. After all, the material object of the book that we hold in our hands seems to tell us that this is precisely the state of things. But if we reflect on this issue for any time at all, we soon come to realize that the physical object of the book is just one (physical) manifestation of the literary text proper. That is to say, the specific novel that we hold in our hands – say, Chinua Achebe's *Things Fall Apart* – is merely one copy (or instantiation) of the literary text itself. Of course, it goes without question that like every other work of fiction *Things Fall Apart* can exist in many different formats and all at the same time (digital, paperback, our memory, and so on); that it can be both the book that I hold in my hands *and* the book that you hold in yours. But how is this possible if Achebe's novel is solely to be understood as a corporeal machine? The answer of course is that it is not possible.

Rather, we have to be conscious of the distinction that we learn to draw early on between the literary text of the novel and the novel as a discrete material form. As a book that we hold in our hands, *Things Fall Apart* is indeed to be regarded as a corporeal form. However, the fact of the matter is that such a book is just one manifestation of the literary text that we call *Things Fall Apart*. It is then the literary text that is incorporeal. Indeed, it is a perfect example of such, for it is endlessly reproducible and presents simultaneously in a number of spatial and temporal locations while retaining its identity (as a book on my bookshelf).

That being said, this brief note on the corporeal form of literary texts does more than just highlight its condition of incorporeality. It also demonstrates well the way in which incorporeal machines like literary texts ultimately destabilize the dualism that threatens to emerge from a consideration of corporeal and incorporeal machines. "All incorporeal machines," Bryant states, "require a corporeal body in order to exist in the world" (2014, 26). And as we have noted, the literary text is no different. Just like any other machine, the literary text is an incorporeal machine that performs transformations on inputs and in so doing produces outputs (Bryant 2014, 38), but it does so through the encounters it has in its physical form. That is to say, the literary text understood as an incorporeal machine encounters other machines of the world only through its myriad discrete corporeal forms. As such, every literary text has the potential to make thousands of individual encounters *at the same time.*

What this notion of the literary text as an incorporeal machine moves us towards is the description of a very particular kind of connectivity – a kind of connectivity that the French philosopher Gilles Deleuze called "rhizomic." The distinctive feature of a rhizomic system is that it does not emanate or begin with a specific point. That is to say, the rhizomic system is without a point of center to which all the other elements of the system are bound. Perhaps the best way to think of this is by considering the difference between trees and grass. Understood in an almost comically simple way, trees begin from their trunk (the single point in the ground) and then, travelling towards the sun, bifurcate in a manner that is well known to biologists – a trunk, some branches, many leaves. Here, the trunk of the tree is the central column of the system, a point upon which all the other elements of the system depend. The trunk supplies the other parts of the tree system with the vital elements necessary for them to function.

The structure of grass, though, is entirely different. Grass does not have this central column. It spreads horizontally rather than vertically, and in so doing abandons the need for a point of center. Indeed, no part of a patch of grass is any more important than any other part of a patch. If I decide to remove a section of grass in order to clear ground for a patio in my garden, the grass to which the section was directly and intimately connected remains unaffected. The same will not be true for a tree that stands in my way. The reason why the grass would remain unaffected is precisely because it lacks the central structure of the tree. In place of a center, grass has given itself over to an unrelenting and haphazard set of connections. Grass connects to itself wherever and whenever it can, and because of this it is best thought of as a substantive multiple – that is, as a plurality that behaves as a particularity.

My point, then, is that we can think of the literary text in much the same way as we think of a patch of grass. Just like a patch of grass, the literary text lacks a central form even though it can boast of a definite edge to its existence. And just as a patch of grass encounters the world through individual blades of grass, so too does the literary text – through the corporealization of the literary text in individual books. Literature and grass are seemingly perfect twins. But this is an image of things that is not without consequence. Indeed, if we are willing to understand the literary text in this way, then it is clear that we must also be willing to be done with the notion of the literary text as a reflection or imitation of the world. Why? Because this account of the incorporeality of literary texts shows that they are not somehow other to, or outside of, or beyond the world that we experience. It shows that they are in fact an integral part of the world. To claim otherwise is born of a certain naivety.

In the first instance, the very fact that literary texts are expressed through language means that they cannot mimic the world. Let us not be fooled into forgetting the rather obvious point that writing is always and only a simple matter of black marks upon a white page. What kind of reflection of a complex world is this? Let us also not forget that Saussure has shown us that language necessarily creates its own sense of things – that because words only make sense within a language-system, they ultimately create their own reality. And in addition to this, let us also not forget (again!) that literature does exactly the same. In what world does life play out as it does in a novel – by setting up a central intrigue, upon which variations are played through a number of acts (which are always significant), that is somehow resolved in the end? Even the great Modernist writers – T.S. Eliot, Virginia Woolf, James Joyce, and so on – who responded to the huge social and political upheavals in Europe around the turn of the twentieth century by giving us the radically fractured text, could not resist the urge to bring the chaotic world under control in the form of a carefully constructed poem or novel. Other critics might argue the point, but even Eliot's extraordinary poem *The Waste Land* (1922), regardless of the polyvocality that gives the poem its fragmentary structure, finally resolves itself. "*Shantih, Shantih, Shantih,*" the final line of the poem announces – a closure that Eliot takes from the ending of each Upanishad, and which means "Peace that surpasses understanding." This then is the poem's resolution: do not look to understand the (chaotic) world; simply try to be at peace with it.

Clearly then, the literary text does not reflect or mimic the world. And it is because of this fact that we should be conscious of not mistaking literature for simply the passive consequence of our being in the world. Rather, literary texts are to be understood as actors in this world. That is to say, they should be recognized for what they are – (incorporeal) machines that function in a very tangible way as part of the world. What I mean by this is that we must recognize that literary texts certainly do impact on, and affect, the world. Perhaps the most obvious example of this is the fact that although texts cannot reflect or imitate the world, they certainly can (and oftentimes do) elicit a range of "real-world" emotions from their readers. Here, the literary text acts in a very palpable way by modifying the sensibility or attitude of its reader. But let us also remember here that because the literary text has a rhizomic connection with the world, it can make itself felt in this way across the entire world. What further evidence do we require of the intimate relationship between literature and the world?

That being said, I do not want to give the impression here that the literary text directs or assumes some kind of primacy in its encounters with other machines. As Deleuze and Guattari write, "there is an aparallel evolution of the book and the world; the book assures the deterritorialization of the world, but the world effects a reterritorialization of the book, which in turn deterritorializes itself in the world" (1999, 11). To the non-specialist, the language used here perhaps confuses more than elucidates, but the point being made is ruthlessly simple – the literary text and the world function as agents of change for each other. That is to say, the literary text affects the world and *vice versa*. This then is no hierarchical model of the relationship between the literary text and the world; it is a horizontal one – one of endless affection or, in other words, endless transformation.

So, if the literary text is a machine then it is an incorporeal machine. And if it is an incorporeal machine then it must connect to the world rhizomically through its physical instantiations. However, the picture this paints of a world of machines effortlessly linking to each other in order to produce various outputs is something of a misleading one. Another assumption that Levi Bryant could have confronted in his list of preconceptions about machines is the belief that all machines either "work" or are "broken." This sense of things is not at all correct. As Bryant himself observes a little later in his book, it seems as though all machines are actually on the verge of breaking down. For Bryant, problems arise when machines come together to form larger machines. While each machine can be connected to another machine in a variety of ways, operationally they remain closed. That is to say, even though a machine may constitute part of the fabric of a larger machine, it will always and only try to act as if it were a singular machine. Because machines act in this way, a certain tension arises between the constitutive machine and the larger machine that ultimately unsettles the function (and therefore the constitution) of the larger machine.

Any organization that we care to talk about will evidence this point for us, so let me take the organization of a university as my example here. The university is as much a machine as any other object in the world. It is of course composed of many other "machines" – most obviously its professors, students, and administrators. Now, what Bryant says is that each of these interior groups (which we might as well call constitutive machines) will operate in a way that only serves their own goals. That is to say, professors will act in a way that benefits the professoriate, students will act in a way that benefits the student body, and the administrators will act in a way that benefits their own agenda. However, because these constitutive machines function in this way, a certain tension will inevitably open up between the private goals of these machines and the private goal pursued by the larger machine – the university. The question is how fatal such tensions will prove to be. The successful university (or at least, the one that continues to stay open for business) is one where the tensions that develop between the constitutive machines and the larger machine do not fatally unsettle its functioning. Conversely, those universities that collapse do so because the tensions that emerge between the interests of the professoriate, the students, and the administrators are so great that they impede the continued functioning of the university. Graham Harman may articulate this observation in terms of an object's fundamental inability to know itself, but that is just another way of saying that "no machine ever manages to totalize or master its parts" (Bryant 2014, 79). In short, although machines can be seen to come together in order to form a larger machine, that larger machine in no way presupposes a perfectly coherent unity.

Where the thought of Harman and Bryant does diverge on this matter is in how they figure what this essential incoherency or inconsistency means for objects and machines. For Harman, the fact that every object withdraws from itself has little effect on the object understood as an object-in-itself – it remains the physical presence of an unsolvable mystery (the mystery being the ontological nature of the object). But for Bryant, the consequence of this picture of the machine is much more dramatic. What it means is that each machine functions with an implicit and inherent set of tensions that constantly threatens to bring about its demise. Put simply, every machine is "perpetually in danger of collapsing or falling apart" (Bryant 2014, 79). After making this point, Bryant turns his attention to other matters and, for me at least, the real significance of what is being intimated is lost. However, if we stress the fact that this observation applies to *all* machines, from the very largest (say, our ecosphere) to the very smallest (the mitochondria in our cells), then what we must conclude from the tensions that inevitably arise from the coupling of machines is that *the world of machines is a world of (imminently) failing machines!*

While this asseveration has the potential to lead us in an untold number of different directions, not least into discussions of entropy and the ordered nature of living organisms, let us re-sharpen our focus here on what this means for the literary text. If it is true that every machine functions on the threshold of failure, then since the literary text is also a machine, it too must be constantly under threat of malfunction or dissolution. This means that we can think of the literary text in a similar manner to that which was outlined by New Criticism – that is, as a "throng of tensions." But unlike the teachings of New Criticism, it is clear that these tensions do not resolve into anything like an "organic unity." Rather the literary text as machine exhibits an interior that never quite meshes together in the expected manner, and that is for the simple reason that it cannot. Again, as machines encounter each other they produce a raft of tensions that will always result in the eventual failure of the larger machine.

We see evidence of such machinic failure in nearly every dimension of the literary text, so let me offer one of the more sweeping or elaborate examples of such failure here – the fact that literature rests on a corruption of sense. One of the interesting points that Timothy Morton makes in his essay "An Object-Oriented Defense of Poetry" (2012) is that literature deals constantly with doubled truths. Consider for example the sentence, "This sentence is false." As Morton explains, this kind of construction is one that has been abandoned to the margins of philosophical thought because of the inability of the discipline to get to grips with the paradoxical nature of the assertion. But acceptance of this doubled truth, or *dialetheia*, is precisely what the literary text demands of its reader. The reader holds in her hands a collection of words from which she is asked to imagine an entire world of meaning. Moreover, even though the world on the page cannot exist – the characters and storylines are, after all, pure invention – it is possible for those fictional worlds and imagined people to have a profound impact on the way in which the reader thinks about and engages with the real world. What this means is that fiction cannot be understood simply as an imagined reality that is aligned with a false reality (for an imagined world, it is assumed, cannot be a "real" or "true" world); it must be understood as something that is both imagined and "true" at the same time. Put simply, the literary text demands that we think of it as both fiction *and* reality – or, to put it in slightly more poetic terms, literature demands that we think of it as a flight of fancy that cannot be anything other than intimately grounded to the world around us.

With the literary text, sense fails – it bifurcates and is drawn towards two radically different conclusions because some of the machinic components of the text pull it towards the realm of the imaginative while other elements insist on its strong relationship to our consensual reality. That is to say, the book/machine is revealed here to be corrupted. But what else could we expect from the marriage of a (Romantic) Idealism that championed the imagination as the best of things and a (hard-nosed) Empiricism that considered the imagination as that which could only "muddle any effort to secure the truth of propositions" (Altieri 2007, 85)? Given that literary critics have known for a good while that every text oscillates between an expression of the world as it is perceived to be (Realism) and an expression of the literary work as an aesthetic object (Postmodernism), we should not be satisfied with our moment of insight here taking the form of an observation that the literary text survives on making a mockery of logic (the complex *dialetheia* of a true fiction of the Real). No. Our moment of insight should rather be drawn from the recognition that despite suffering spectacularly from a failure to observe the law of non-contradiction – of demonstrating that literature is at the same time both fictional and true – the literary text retains its potential to affect its reader precisely because it falters in this way. In other words, it is the fact that the literary text fails to reconcile the different directions in which sense travels through it that ultimately gives it the power to affect its reader in far-reaching and unexpected ways.

The significance of this observation cannot be over-estimated, for it intimates something profound about the operation of all machines. It says: the world of machines may be a world of failing machines, but it is the very failure of such machines that makes possible the birth of "the new." I will talk more about the mechanics of this birth of the new in the following chapters, so let me offer here just a brief discussion of the coordinates by which one can quickly get to grips with the relationship between machinic failure and what is essentially the moment of creativity: Viktor Shklovsky, defamiliarization, and the year 1917.

In 1917, the Russian literary critic Viktor Shklovsky published a quite remarkable essay which is known today in English as "Art as Technique" (or, less commonly, "Art as Device"). In this essay, Shklovsky argued that the language of literature is our language of the everyday "defamiliarized." That is to say, the language that we find in novels and poetry is one of a curious variety – a language whose only purpose is to try and make the common world we see around us appear somehow unfamiliar or odd. Such estrangement of the reader from the familiar world happens, Shklovsky claims, because the language of literature breaks what is the automatic functioning of our day-to-day perception of the world. Put simply, the language we find in literature compels the reader to think longer over what is being said, what is being represented or expressed in the text, and in this way it interrupts the habitualized (we might as well say, "unthinking") way in which we mostly navigate the world. As Shklovsky puts it,

Habitualization devours works, clothes, furniture, one's wife, and the fear of war [...] Art exists that one may recover the sensation of life; it exists to make one feel things, to make the stone *stony*. (Shklovsky 1965, 12)

For Shklovsky, life tends towards unthinking repetition – we are creatures of habit who will tend to repeat the same behaviors or repeat the same way of thinking about things until something jolts us from this passive slumber. And it is precisely this that the best literature does. Literature, Shklovsky claims, has the potential to recover the sensation of a life to be lived, by rendering the world that we think we know in unusual or unfamiliar ways. In other words, what makes literature "literary" is that it makes the reader experience and think about the world anew. As Shklovsky says, literature exists in order to make the reader experience what we might call the "artfulness of the stone," rather than the stone regarded as that simple object on the ground, "over there."

There are many ways by which literature can interrupt the process of habitualization, but for Shklovsky the great Russian novelist Leo Tolstoy demonstrates better than most how easily such defamiliarization can be effected. What is special about Tolstoy is the way in which he repeatedly "describes an object as if he were seeing it for the first time, an event as if it were happening for the first time" (Shklovsky 1965, 13). He does so by refusing to name specific objects or events, opting instead to describe them without resorting to words that are closely aligned to the object or event under discussion. In this way, the reader is made to dwell on the text until it is she who has resolved the disparate images given on the page into a coherent picture of something specific.

It is, then, this slow perception of things that is inaugurated through the process of defamiliarization, which for Shklovsky reinvigorates our "sensation of life," and for us describes the relationship between machinic failure and the spark of creativity. What Shklovsky clearly shows in this early essay is that the language of literature *intentionally fails* to mesh with the reader's experience of the everyday, and it is precisely this failure that makes the reader see the world in new and interesting ways. An easy analogy can be drawn here that makes the point crystal-clear – just like Heidegger's hammer, which only comes to our attention once it is damaged and therefore unfit for purpose, the literary text only affects the reader as it breaks down. Our impulse might be to fix a failing machine, but to do so would be to live forever in a world without the new.

5

The Reading Machine

However, Viktor Shklovsky teaches us about more than just the machinic nature of the literary text. Indeed, he teaches us that if the literary text is a machine then so too is the reader because, in the act of reading, the text and reader form a sympathetic unity which cannot easily be prised apart. This, then, is what we should take away from his description of the way in which great literature antagonizes our habitual account of things – that is, the recognition that it is we, the readers, who stutter through an encounter with a stuttering text. So, when Tolstoy describes an object as if he were seeing it for the first time, he does so, according to Shklovsky, in a way that unsettles not only the text but also the automatic interpretive processes of the reader. "How best," Shklovsky would imagine Tolstoy asking himself, "to throw into tension the relationship between an object and the reader's lived-experience of that same object?" And with this question the intimate relationship between text and reader is exposed – that what Shklovsky called "the roughening of language" (1965, 24) actually results in the roughening (or interference) of the way in which a reader encounters a text.

Put another way, the proper concern of Shklovsky has always been the nexus of reader and text, for he recognized early on the fundamental relationship between the two. Yet – and here is the problem – it is true to say that Shklovsky never explained in any great detail the mechanics of this relationship. Sure, he offered great insights into particular aspects of the relationship, but he never painted it with anything other than the broadest of brush strokes. It is this task then that this chapter takes up. It asks, "What is the character of the machinic encounter between text and reader, and what results from it?" Of course, questions such as these can only be answered properly if we first understand from where they emerge. To this end, we must begin by recognizing the wider significance of Shklovsky's work to literary criticism.

Shklovsky's insistence on the concern for the reader stands as the proper precursor to a turn in literary criticism that would come to understand that it is the reader who ultimately brings literary works to life. Without the reader, a text is permanently locked up within itself – it cannot communicate; it cannot affect those around it; it cannot "speak." Understood like this, the unread text is best regarded as a packet of potential. Even those disciples of the supposedly objective critical art of New Criticism had to finally concede that, as Cleanth Brooks admitted, "no one in his right mind could forget the reader. He is essential for 'realizing' any poem or novel" (1995, 87)[11] – which is to say, the reader is vital to bringing the literary work into being.

Indeed, what a new generation of European and American scholars were discovering in the mid-twentieth century was that the little-considered figure of the reader, who in the Romantic Humanist tradition had always been thought of as the passive imbiber of an author's deeply profound observations about the world of men, was fundamental to understanding the relationship between literary texts and meaning. It had always been supposed that the literary text conveyed the author's meaning in a fairly transparent way, but those who came to be known as the Reader-Response critics challenged this understanding in nearly every way. For these critics, it was the literary and life experiences that a reader brought to a text that largely determined the character of the meaning of the text itself. Of course, some critics were more conservative than others in the way in which they conceptualized the relationship between text and reader, but nonetheless each stressed the significant role that the reader played in accounting for the meaning of a literary work.

One of the most notable writers of this kind of criticism was the German literary theorist and critic Wolfgang Iser. For Iser, the literary text as it presented itself could be thought of in two ways. First, a text could be considered in terms of its "artistry," which is to say that certain style of expression and intent that the author brings to the written text. Second, a text could be thought of in terms of its "esthetics," which for Iser means the way in which a reader makes use of, or interprets, the literary text in front of him. Yet, it is between these two poles of the text, Iser argues, that the actual literary work emerges. That is to say, Iser thinks of the literary work as the constant negotiation between the intention of the author, which is actualized by the words on the page, and what he calls the reader's disposition, by which he means "the kaleidoscope of perspectives, preintentions, and recollections" of the reader (Iser 1972, 284). In this way, the literary work, which is to say the literary text that is understood to exhibit some kind of meaning, inhabits a "virtual" realm between these "real" poles. In short, the literary work exists between the reader and the text.

What leads Iser to such a position is the persuasive account of the way in which sentences work together in the literary text given by the Polish philosopher Roman Ingarden. For Ingarden, sentences link up in a number of interesting ways to form complex units of meaning that ultimately give rise to the genres of the written text. But they do so only to the extent that the sentences invite input from readers. Sentences cannot simply make assertions about things; they must also gesture beyond what is actually said, and in so doing they must always signal something that is "to come." Understood like this, sentences are "components" which simultaneously rehearse what has been *and* prefigure that which is yet to come for the reader. This is what Ingarden referred to as the "sentence-thought" of a piece of writing – the retrospective and anticipatory quality of the sentence that is locked into the literary text.

Where Iser departs from Ingarden's account of things is in how he treats the moment of interruption to the seemingly effortless flow of sentence-thought. For Ingarden, disruption to the gentle oscillation of sentence-thought is a mark of a flawed text – a moment where the illusory quality of the written work is suddenly brought to the attention of the reader and the immersive spell of literature is fatally broken. But for Iser, such disruptions were much more than this. What Ingarden saw as a flaw in the literature, Iser saw as sitting at the heart of all literature. In his influential essay "The Reading Process" (1972), Iser writes:

> And yet literary texts are full of unexpected twists and turns, and frustration of expectations. Even in the simplest story there is bound to be some kind of blockage, if only because no tale can ever be told in its entirety. Indeed, it is only through inevitable omissions that a story gains its dynamism. (1972, 284)

What Iser is saying here is that literature does not look to reconcile moments of interruption in its sentence-thought; it actively tries to encourage these moments of discontinuity. It does so because these challenging aspects of a text engage the reader by asking her to consciously reconcile the interruptions by drawing on her own literary or lived experience. He continues, to engage the text in this way is "to bring into play our own faculty for establishing connections – for filling in the gaps left by the text itself" (Iser 1972, 285), and thus the significance of the reader's role in the literary act is revealed. Indeed, it is the fact that each reader draws on her own disposition or experiences to fill these gaps of a text that accounts for the many different readings that any text can seemingly support. This, then, is why we can read the same text twice but get very different readings each time – it is not the text that has changed between readings but rather our own experiences that we bring to it. For this reason, we must conclude with Iser that "one text is potentially capable of several different realizations, and no reading can ever exhaust the full potential, for each reader will fill in the gaps in his own way, thereby excluding the various other possibilities" (1972, 285).

Yet, there is a danger that the literary text will demand too much work from the reader. T.S. Eliot's *The Waste Land* (1922) is a great poem, and one that demands a great deal of attention from its reader in terms of connecting images and voices in order to produce a reading of the poem. But while for the literary scholar the poem stands as a formidable challenge, one in which the critic revels as she traces and brings into conversation seemingly disparate themes and images, for others the poem perhaps demands a little too much. For example, even before one gets to the first line of the poem – surely one of the most notorious first lines in twentieth-century poetry, "April is the cruellest month" – the reader is presented with this:

"*Nam Sibyllam quidem Cumis ego ipse oculis meis vidi in ampulla pendere, et cum illi pueri dicerent: Σιβυλλα τι θελεις; respondebat illa: αποθανειν θελω.*"

For Ezra Pound
il miglior fabbro.

How is your Latin, your Ancient Greek, and your Italian? The literary scholar will spend time decoding this epigraph, and in so doing will learn that the Latin and Greek passage comes to us from Petronius's play, *The Satyricon*. She will learn that the passage translates into English like this: "I saw with my own eyes the Sibyl of Cumae hanging in a jar, and when the boys said to her, Sibyl, what do you want? she replied I want to die." Taken in association with Eliot's sign of deference to Ezra Pound – *il miglior fabbro* ("the better craftsman") – for the critic the tone of the poem is set. But for those who do not commit to this kind of literary archaeology, which is to say the recovery of Petronius's *The Satyricon* or indeed Dante's *The Divine Comedy* from which Eliot takes his dedication to Pound, the epigraph alone is enough to irremediably distance the reader.[12] For Iser, what is happening when the reader feels detached from the text in hand is that the gap between the "artistic text" and the "esthetic text" has become too great. Unable to draw on our own literary or lived experienced in order to reconcile these two aspects of the literary work, the reader comes to think of the text in hand as an incoherent whole, and for this reason she rejects it as either "too difficult" or simply as something that is "unreadable."

The flip-side to this situation, as Iser tells us, is that rather than being too difficult, the literary text in front of us might actually not be demanding enough. That is to say, the text we read might not do enough to challenge our expectations, or to surprise us from time to time. In this circumstance, Iser says that the reader will become quickly bored with the "obvious and unchallenging" narrative, and therefore commit it to the same pile of unread books on which *The Waste Land* might find itself. The point is therefore that the discontinuities of a literary text must be carefully choreographed – if there is either too much or too little dislocation (or "surprise") with the reader's literary and lived experiences, the result will be a disengagement of the reader. The common analogy that is made to capture the sense of this takes us once again to the realm of machines. The spark plug, which ignites the fuel that powers our cars, has a very precisely engineered gap between central and lateral electrodes across which a spark must arc if it is to "fire." Naturally, if the gap is too great then the spark will inevitably fail to arc between the electrodes. Similarly, if the gap is too small then the system will be permanently shorted, meaning that the spark plug will again fail. For exactly the same reason, Iser argued that the literary text must present its inconsistencies, its blockages, its challenges to sentence-thought within a range of tolerance, or risk being forever dismissed by the reader.

Although Iser would not have gone this far, the logic of reader-response criticism resolves into a certain provocation to which the French semiotician Roland Barthes responded in his rightly celebrated essay "The Death of the Author" (1967). If, as Iser and his colleagues maintained, it is the reader who ultimately produces the meaning of a text (the reader writes the text as she reads), then surely the Author is something of an unnecessary figure in the act of literature. What is the need for a presiding figure of authority outside of the text, one might rightly ask, if it is the reader's literary and lived experience (no matter how rich or poor that experience) that eventually comes to determine the significance of the text? What Barthes did in his essay was to take this image of a frail Author arrived at through the logic of reader-response criticism and show us all why he was not long for this world!

Arguing that the very idea of an Author is an unnecessary complication to understanding the production of literature that comes to us through the discovery of "the prestige of the individual" in the late Middle Ages, Barthes explains that the etymology of the word "text" tells us all we need to know about the proper position of the Author in relation to the act of literature. "Text" emerges from the Latin word *texere*, which means to weave, to join, to fit together, to braid, to interweave, to construct or fabricate. In this sense, our literary texts are not singular but rather woven objects that arise from the act of threading together written forms. Barthes puts it like this: "A text [...] is a multi-dimensional space in which a variety of writings, none of them original, blend and clash: the text is a tissue of quotations" (1977, 143). Eliot's *The Waste Land* is again an excellent example here. The poem draws on a huge and diverse range of literature in order to compose its images. In just the first section alone one can note the direct influence of Chaucer's *Canterbury Tales* (1475), Wagner's *Tristan und Isolde* (1865), and Baudelaire's *Fleurs du Mal*

(1857). But these literary allusions and inheritances sit on top of a poem that is itself structured by the Arthurian legend of the Fisher King – the king whose fleshy wound not only affects his body but also the fecundity of his land and people.

It is in this sense that Barthes maintained that no text is original, for it is clear that every text inexorably inherits its style, form, genre, and language, and so on, from what preceded it. For this reason, Barthes states that "the writer can only imitate a gesture that is always anterior, never original." That is to say, the writer's only power "is to mix writings, to counter the ones with the others, in such a way as never to rest on any one of them" (Barthes 1977, 143). Read in this way, what we had traditionally called the Author is *at best* an Orchestrator, which is to say a compositor rather than a creator. At worst, the figure of the Author is an anachronism – a keeper of secrets from whom we are all liberated in his absence.

In this way, Barthes' assertion leads to one of the few truisms of literary studies – that literature is always and only a local event. In other words, literature only comes into being once it has been read by a specific reader. Before this act of engagement, the literary text can only be thought of in terms of potential; something akin to Schrödinger's unfortunate cat. "What," we ask ourselves as we turn a book over in our hands, glancing at the front and back covers, "does this book have in store for us?" Of course, the only way to find out is to read the book! But this obvious statement means that we cannot do anything other than recognize the profound role that the reader plays in the event of literature. The important literary critic Derek Attridge puts it like this,

It is the reader – not as free-floating subject but as the nexus of a number of specific histories and contextual formations – who brings the work into being, differently each time, in a singular performance of the work not so much written as writing. (2004, 9)

Without a reader, the text remains "unactualized," a purely abstract, virtual form, a literal unknown. However, there is something else of importance to note here. We have already spent some time discussing the analytical practice of over-mining, and it seems to me that Attridge's characterization of the reader runs perilously close to repeating this style of analysis. For example, in this passage Attridge gives us the sense that he is willing to abandon the idea of the reader as an individual to a discussion of the complex social, historical, and political contexts that come to situate her. Yet, this is not at all the sense that we are given of the act of reading. Indeed, Attridge stresses the fact that reading is "a singular performance of the work," which is to say a unique, never-to-be-repeated event. To my mind at least, what Attridge says of reading must also apply to the reader. After all, how can a reading be unique if the reader herself is not also understood as unique? To claim such a singular position for every reader is a radical one, but one that means we can go on to account for the individual, locally specific readings that are carried out on texts. If the reader (and text for that matter) is only understood through the various contexts in which she sits then we lose the ability to discriminate between the local and the universal, and as Graham Harman warns:

A completely interconnected cosmos would have no individual location at all: everything would affect everything else, and all things would be mutually and utterly near [...] For there to be location, there must also be individuality, however ephemeral and mutable it may be. (2012, 195)

The point is that it is vital to think of readers as individual, discrete forms. To do otherwise, as Harman argues, is to make the world grind to a halt. So, the reader encounters the text in a unique way, just like every other object encounters the world in a profoundly individual way. And what makes such encounters possible is the distance between objects, which arises from the fact that objects are discrete, unique forms.

However, given this state of things, it is true that the encounter between the reader and the literary text is not adequately reflected in the Iserian vision of the constant negotiation between the "horizons of the text" and the "horizons of the reader." What we need therefore is a new vision of the event of literature, and this is precisely what our machine-oriented discussion of the reader and the literary text offers. Ours is a vision of machines coming together in order to read – the reader-as-machine coupling with the literary text/machine. The question is, then, what does such a coupling of machines look like and what results from it?

In this first instance, it is clear that what we are talking about are "assemblages." That is to say, an assemblage describes the resultant coupling of machines. Now, since all machines are always composed of yet smaller machines, it is true that all machines are already assemblages. Take, for example, us. The work of Roy Sleator and others has shown that the vast majority of what we think of as the human body is in fact anything other than "human." Sleator explains:

Bacteria occupy all surfaces of the human body with a combined microbial cell population ~10 times that of human cells, a fact which, in essence, makes us more microbe than man! The human colon (large intestine) for example, has been identified as the most densely populated natural bacterial ecosystem, encompassing more bacterial cells than all of our microbial communities combined. The total number of genes encoded by their collective genomes (referred to as the gut microbiome) is at least one order of magnitude greater than the human genome. (2010, 214)

This fact is startling, but it only hints at the complexity of the human thought of as a "superorganism," which is to say as a vast community of life. The work of Peter Kramer and Paola Bressan, for example, has shown amongst other things that microbes in our brains and guts can and do change our behavior, and that many of us carry the cells of other human beings in our brains (Kramer and Bressan 2015). As the extraordinary Donna Haraway once quipped, from this one should perhaps take comfort from the fact that when we die only a tiny fraction of the DNA that is put into the ground with our body will have ever belonged to "us." But there is also a serious point to be made here. If, as Kramer and Bressan state, microbes can do our thinking for us and DNA from other (non-present) humans routinely appears in our brains, then it must be true that we do not think as individuals. Rather, we think as "we," which is to say as the result of the (messy) convergence and tensions that arise between the impulses of the biosphere that describes our body. This is the human body as assemblage.

And in just the same way, it is true that the literary text is also an assemblage. Barthes's "The Death of the Author" begins with a comment on the number of "voices" that are present in any one text – the voices of the author, narrator, and characters for sure, but also the voices of specific social dialects or turns of phrase associated with particular professions or industries (certainly, commerce has a language that is entirely different to that of high fashion), and others:

In his story *Sarrasine*, Balzac [...] writes this sentence: "It was Woman, with her sudden fears, her irrational whims, her instinctive fears, her unprovoked bravado, her daring and her delicious delicacy of feeling." Who is speaking in this way? Is it the story's hero, concerned to ignore the castrato concealed beneath the woman? Is it the man Balzac, endowed by his personal experience with a philosophy of Woman? Is it the author Balzac, professing certain "literary" ideas of femininity? Is it universal wisdom? or romantic psychology?

It will always be impossible to know, for the good reason that all writing is itself this special voice, consisting of several indiscernible voices. (1977, 142)

Once we then go on to understand that these socio-ideological voices can persist in language and present in our own use of language, we have a good idea of what Mikhail Bakhtin called the "heteroglossic text" – a multi-voiced text that stands as the result of realizing that we are born into a language that existed a long time before us. Ours is a language with a social history that is captured in the word or the phrase, and it is this history – the recorded voice of all those who have used the word – that presents itself, consciously or (most commonly) otherwise, through our use of the language. Understood like this, we do not speak language; it speaks us. This is the literary text understood as assemblage.

It is then these assemblages which we have learned to call "the reader" and "the text" that come together in the act of reading. But when these assemblages encounter each other they do so not at arm's length, but rather as a coupling – that is, as a coming-together that forms an entirely new assemblage. It is this assemblage of the reader and text that I want to call here the "reading machine." Like Heidegger's observation about the collapse of the subject/object principle as we employ certain tools to accomplish particular tasks, at the birth of the reading machine the distinction between reader and text evaporates. It does so because the reading machine simply cannot exist in any other state than the one that sees the reader and the text come together in the act of reading. In short, if there is no reader or no text, then there can be no reading machine. It is this fact that explains why the collapse of the subject/object principle within the reading machine is not reliant on the act of reading being a subconscious performance (as it is for Heidegger's tool-analysis). For the reading machine, there simply can be no subject/object principle in place, whether or not one is cognizant of the individual components of the larger assemblage. In precisely the same way that a bicycle without its wheels is not a bicycle, neither is the reading machine without the literary text or the reader.

For this reason, we have to take to task the way in which the Reader-Response critics characterize the encounter between reader and text. As Iser made clear, our encounter with a literary text (hopefully) opens up a semantic void that we are compelled to fill in with our own literary and lived experiences. But this cannot describe the character of the coupling of machines. If one understands reading as the product of a machinic assemblage then those voids of comprehension that Ingarden, Iser, and others have postulated are better thought of as expressions of exactly the kind of tensions that one would expect to see arise between machines that are functioning within a larger machine. As we discussed in the previous chapter, all machines function for themselves rather than for the larger assemblage. This means that all machines function with an implicit tension raging between the direction in which constitutive machines wish to pull and the direction in which the larger assemblage of machines wishes to move. So it is that the discontinuities and blockages of a literary text that Iser attributes to a problem in the relationship between reader and text is actually the expected result of the inevitable internal tension that develops between components of the reading machine. As such, it is clear that the literary work does not take place in some virtual realm between reader and text, as Iser would have it. Rather, the literary work emerges as the product of the tensions that are implicit to the act of reading or, put another way, as the result of the inevitable misfiring of the reading machine.

And there is more. When a reader and a text come together to form a reading machine, the assemblage acts to change the way in which the reader thinks about and therefore behaves in the world. In addition to the scientific evidence for this claim, every one of us can give an anecdote about a particular novel or a particular poem that had a profound impact on the way in which we conducted ourselves in the world.[13] Perhaps a novel changed our mind about a particular issue or introduced us to some previously unknown idea or confirmed one of our wild suspicions. Perhaps it did something else to us, but to talk in this way about a novel is to recognize the fact that literary works do have the capacity to change us in some way. Of course, the dramatic interventions are easier to recall than those so-called "minor moments," but it is true that *every* text we read (even this one!) will somehow affect the way in which we behave in the world, no matter whether that change is effectively imperceptible or, on the other end of the scale, marks a radical schism in our thinking or behavior.

From this we learn that the reading machine is quite different to those machines that come together to form it – that is, the reader/machine and the literary text/machine. Indeed, how could it not be, given that the primary function of the reading machine is to change the way in which the reader thinks about the world? But this willingness to distinguish between the reading machine and the reader/machine and the literary text/machine brings with it its own problems. Since every machine is constituted by ever smaller machines, it is clear that we have to think seriously about the point at which a machinic assemblage becomes a new machine in and of itself rather than as a collection of other, smaller machines.

Levi Bryant explains the process by which a new machine is born by examining the properties of water. First, he says, let us think of water as a machine made of three smaller machines – two hydrogen machines and an oxygen machine, which we all learned to denote in school like this: H_2O. Understood like this, it would seem sensible to conclude that water, as an assemblage of hydrogen and oxygen, would simply inherit its characteristics from its "parents." But this is not at all the case. In fact, even the most cursory examination of the properties of water shows the obvious ways in which it acts in the world very differently to either hydrogen or oxygen atoms. Perhaps the most immediate difference between water and its component parts is that at room temperature water is a liquid whereas hydrogen and oxygen are not (thankfully, or we should all be a little bit more like fish than we already are).[14] For this reason, water tends to quench most fires whereas hydrogen and oxygen would only exacerbate things. Our chemistry books not only teach us that water has a greater density than either hydrogen or oxygen but that it also reacts in a very different way to certain temperature gates – water freezes at 0°C whereas the freezing point of hydrogen and oxygen is –259 °C and –219 °C, respectively. The list of differences is, of course, nearly endless, but the point is well-made – water, that thing that emerges from the coming together of hydrogen and oxygen atoms, is very different to those constitutive elements. It is, then, the fact that water acts in the world in a way that its parts as individual machines cannot that means it has become a new machine rather than a conglomeration of "simpler" machines.

Importantly, what is true of water is also true of the reading machine. In just the same way that water changes the capacity of hydrogen and oxygen to act in the world, the reading machine changes the way in which the reader herself encounters the world. The question of exactly how the reading machine does so is an extraordinarily complicated one, but one that I think we can begin to unfold if we just change the direction from which we address the question. To this end, let us consider literary censorship.

In addition to being a simple act of prohibition, the censorship of literature is also a clear record of the way in which powerful institutions regard the act of reading. For the establishment, reading is a Janus-faced activity. On the one hand, reading the "right kind" of literature can unite a people – post-colonial revolutionary leaders, for example, sought to rebuild nations that had been ravaged by ethnic division in the wars of independence by calling for a kind of literature that showed a precolonial past in which people of every ethnic group lived together peacefully and prosperously. But on the other hand, reading the "wrong kind" of literature can lead to a radical destabilization of the status quo. As Ray Bradbury makes clear in *Fahrenheit 451*, since reading holds the potential to encourage the reader to think in challenging and confrontational ways about the world in which she lives, it is reading that precedes every kind of revolutionary action. It is, then, for this reason that those in power seek to restrict the propagation of what they consider to be the "wrong kind" of literature. To try to head-off the formation of certain reading machines is to head-off the possibility of revolutionary action.

But understood like this, such negative engagement with the reading machine, which is after all the premise for every act of literary censorship, demonstrates clearly one of the important ways that a reading machine modifies the reader's encounter the world. The reading machine provokes new ideas in the reader. That is to say, it stimulates that core faculty known as the imagination, which Alfred North Whitehead considered so vital to intellectual advancement. Yet, it is the fact that the State fears this firing of the imagination (and so tries to inhibit the formation of certain reading machines) that is important to us here because it means that there must be more to the imagination than we previously thought. Indeed, what the State fears is not so much the firing of the imagination but rather the way in which the musings of the imagination can transform into real physical action. Put simply, the State recognizes that the imagination is not something that is only linked up to an ephemeral world of dreaming (as it is commonly supposed); it is also intimately linked up to the way in which we physically experience the world.

Of course, this is precisely Harvard philosopher Richard Moran's point when he writes that our imagination is absolutely vital to the operation of our memories and desires. He explains, "most of the suffering and satisfaction in life takes place either *prior* to the expected events that are supposed to deliver the real goods; or after the fact, savored in remembrance or sticking in one's craw, as the case may be" (1994, 78). Imagination tempers our memories and our desires, and when they come together in service of questioning what we see they do so as a heady concoction with the potential to set us on the path of very tangible acts of rebellion (if not revolution). If this sounds familiar that is because it is. What is being described here is the way in which every reading machine exhibits the potential to swell the appetite of its reader for utopian thinking. When our memories (which we use to contextualize our sense of the world in which we find ourselves) meet our desires (which inevitably direct us towards the future and questions of what this world could be like), the radical character of the reading machine and the way in which it changes how we encounter the world is revealed. Imagination stimulates action – the proper power of the reading machine is its ability to foment revolutionary thought and action.

The really worrying thing for centers of power like the State and the Church, though, is the way in which the (utopian and therefore revolutionary) reading machine persists even after one has supposedly finished reading. Although a reading machine can be prevented from forming by ensuring that a reader never encounters a text, once it has been formed it does not immediately collapse when its constitutive machines are pulled apart. That is to say, reading machines are not dependent on the continued physical proximity of reader and text. Even when we put a book down on the side table or return it to the bookshelf, the reading machine itself stays intact. This seems counter-intuitive, but in order to understand why this is indeed the case we have to remember that the literary text is an incorporeal machine. This means that the literary text is not reliant on the physical form of the book in order to continue to act in and on the world. Put simply, the book stays with us long after we have finished handling it. For sure, the coupling of the reading machine may be a little more tenuous than before – without question, we forget certain aspects of those texts that we have supposedly finished reading – but the reader/text assemblage of the reading machine continues to function precisely because of the rhizomic connection between text and reader. In short, we continue to make sense of a literary text even after we have supposedly finished reading it.

All of this means that the reading machine is a very remarkable machine indeed – an assemblage that does not rely on the continuity of a physical coupling in order to radically change the way in which its reader encounters the world. But nonetheless, this is how I want to think about the literary critic reading the literary text. So, in the next chapter we take this machinic coupling as our object of study. Our question is, what can such a reading machine *do*? As we know, it is the only sensible question that one can ask of machines. It is in offering some tentative answers to this question that we disassemble and reorganize contemporary ideas about what the literary critic does. In considering the kinds of transformation of inputs that flow through the reading machine and the sheer variety of outputs that they produce, we ultimately identify what we might think of as an object-oriented reading practice.

6

A Reading Practice

Almost immediately after outlining the principles of his object-oriented philosophy, Graham Harman was asked to consider how his findings might impact on other areas of study. While being largely deferential on the matter, saying that he preferred others to explore the possible affect and effect of speculative realism on areas of academic interest outside of his own, it seemed that Harman could not resist the lure of literary studies. Indeed, I think it is fair to say that of all those engaged with speculative realism, Harman has been the most active in debates concerning the world of literature. This chapter looks at Harman's engagement with literary studies as well as the forays of others, and submits them to critique. In so doing, my intention is to highlight a reading practice by which I think a literary critic who is sympathetic to the tenets of an object-oriented philosophy can conduct a sustained literary criticism. If such a thing as a speculative-realist literary criticism is to exist, then my argument is that it should look something like what follows.

Let us begin then with Graham Harman's thoughts on literature and literary criticism. Always mindful of the way in which objects seemingly dissolve as they are "mined" in the act of interpretation, Harman anchors his notion of a revisionary literary criticism with this single point of interest. In his essay "The Well-Wrought Broken Hammer" (2012), Harman argues that literary criticism should dedicate itself to the task of exposing the way in which specific texts "resist such dissolution" (2012, 200). Put simply, it is the job of the literary critic to demonstrate the thresholds at which a text ceases to be itself – that is, the point at which we can no longer recognize, say, *Great Expectations* (1861) as the novel *Great Expectations*. The way in which one should do

this, Harman says, is by undertaking a radical act that intentionally modifies the text in hand. That is to say, what Harman
wants the literary critic to do in order to test the thresholds of a
literary text is to directly interfere with it. In other words, he
wants the literary critic to challenge the holism of a text by
actually adding or removing sections to it. Only in this way,
Harman argues, will we find those moments when a specific
literary work stops being the text that we recognize. And when
we find these thresholds, the essential character of the text itself
will be discernible in such a way that we will be able to announce
with absolute certainty statements such as, "*Great Expectations*
cannot survive as a text in itself without this word/this sentence/
this passage." Taking Herman Melville's nineteenth-century
classic *Moby-Dick* (1851) as his example, Harman writes:

> Instead of just writing about *Moby-Dick*, why not try short-
> ening it to various degrees in order to discover the point at
> which it ceases to sound like *Moby-Dick*? Why not imagine it
> lengthened even further, or told by a third-person narrator
> rather than Ishmael, or involving a cruise in the opposite
> direction around the globe? (2012, 202)

One can almost hear the gasps of the literary critics who hear this
for the first time. For most, such a suggestion can only lead to
unforgiveable acts of literary vandalism – something akin to
drawing a moustache on the Mona Lisa while at the same time
refusing to acknowledge the irony invested in the act![15] But I am
sure that what Harman has in mind here is the literary equiv-
alent of Husserl's project to reach the essential qualities or
aspects of an object – that is, to strip away the dispensable
qualities of an object as it presents itself in the world at a
particular moment in order to see only the fundamental qualities
that the object needs "in order to be what it is" (Harman 2012,
186). Think here of how the qualities of a bird are multiplied by

trying to capture a sense of that same bird as it is on the wing (its aspect to us, its speed, its color, and so on).

However, it is precisely this kind of provenance to Harman's thoughts on reading literature here that I think accounts for the shortcomings of this kind of direct textual modification as a style of literary criticism. Undoubtedly, the exercise would be an interesting one – one that could show that "*Moby-Dick* differs from its own exact length and its own modifiable plot details, and is […] able to survive certain modifications and not others" (Harman 2012, 202). But clearly this is more about scoring points in philosophy departments than it is about reading Melville's novel. Indeed, if we were to be slightly uncharitable, we could say that this species of literary modification is only useful as a critical approach to literature to the extent that it helps the literary critic understand better both Husserl's analytical method and Harman's insistence on the literary text as an object in its own right. Moreover, it would appear that this kind of manipulation of a text strikes at the very core of thinking about the literary text as an object in itself. I struggle to imagine how this is different in principle to chipping pieces off a particular stone in order to get a better sense of its "stoniness" or, at the other end of the spectrum, gluing pieces of stone together for the same purpose. For these reasons, as a way of thinking with texts, direct literary modification is for me at best a curio rather than the basis of a robust new reading strategy.

Yet, I do not want to suggest that all acts of literary modification are useless to the critic. In fact, *indirect* literary modification is a different proposition altogether. Later in the same passage that encourages us to get our scissors out and play collage with literary works, Harman goes on to ask, "Why not imagine that a letter by Shelley was actually written by Nietzsche, and consider the resulting consequences and *lack* of consequences?" (2012, 202). The point here is to decontextualize literary works, to see what happens when texts, as Eileen Joy puts it, "are not constrained by either their most manifest properties or their so-called historical environments" (2013, 33). To decontextualize the text in this way is both an effort to liberate literary criticism from the *obligation* of socio-political commentary and an invitation to consider the product of supposedly unrelated literary works coming together. In other words, it is to read in a way that refuses to give privilege to the environment in which a text was composed in favor of "critical play" (Joy 2013, 33). To do so, as Jorge Luis Borges's infamous invention Pierre Menard concludes, is to invest the most ordinary literary work with a sense of adventure:

Menard [...] has enriched, by means of new technique, the halting and rudimentary art of reading: this new technique is one of the deliberate anachronism and the erroneous attribution. This technique, whose applications are infinite, prompts us to go through the *Odyssey* as if it was posterior to the *Aeneid* and the book *Le jardin du Centaure* of Madame Henri Bachelier as if it were by Madame Henri Bachelier. This technique fills the most placid works with adventure. (Borges 2000, 71)

For me, this species of indirect literary modification holds much promise as the basis of a new reading strategy, for the simple fact is that it captures perfectly what actually happens in the formation of every reading machine. When we read a literary work we do so influenced by what we have previously read. That is to say, we typically read texts out of chronological order – *Gravity's Rainbow* (1973) followed by *The Moonstone* (1868); *Catch-22* (1961) followed by the *Adventures of Huckleberry Finn* (1884). In this way, later texts influence our sense of an earlier text all the time. Similarly, it is my experience that we rarely share the same geographical space as the literary work – I sit here in Hong Kong reading work by the Mozambican writer Mia Couto, the

American Philip K. Dick, and the Argentinian Borges. To this extent, we can say that we read both anachronistically and in a properly utopian fashion (in the sense that we do not share our physical location with the literary work). As such, Menard's technique is not foreign to us. Rather, it is characteristic of how we actually experience texts. What *is* foreign to us as "common readers" (to borrow Virginia Woolf's term for "the non-critic," "the non-scholar") is the imposition of an academic apparatus that insists that certain literary works cannot be read together or cannot be read anachronistically. Let us be done with such impositions, because ultimately they can only inhibit what we can do with literature. If we are to honor Menard's "new technique," we must do so by enlivening as many ways of reading texts as possible.

But at the same time, let us not also be unduly influenced by the lure of "the weird." What unites Harman's and Joy's perceptions of a literary criticism inflected by the concerns of object-oriented philosophy is the fetishization of "the weird" or "the uncanny." And there are of course good reasons why both Harman and Joy center their critical practice on the weird – not least because it seems to inhabit that space between the noumenal and phenomenal planes that so interests the speculative realist. Yet, as a description of a text, that is as something "fatally torn between its deeper reality and its accidents, relations, and qualities" (Joy 2013, 29), the weird always has its end-limit. That is to say, the weird always reaches a point where we can only say that what we have witnessed is the human (mind) failing to project its mastery over the world of things. Let me take Harman's favorite author of the weird, the notorious American writer H.P. Lovecraft, as my example of such. In this well-known passage from "The Call of Cthulhu," the primordial force of Cthulhu is rising from the deep to make its presence felt once again in the world of men:

Three men were swept up by the flabby claws before anybody turned [...] Parker slipped as the other three were plunging frenziedly over endless vistas of green-crusted rock to the boat, and Johansen swears he was swallowed up by an angle of masonry which shouldn't have been there; an angle which was acute, but behaved as if it were obtuse. (Lovecraft 1999, 167)

The sense of an unknown object, incomprehensible to the human mind (conceptually incomprehensible to the human mind – "an angle which was acute, but behaved as if it were obtuse") yet acting on the human in a very real way, is obviously important to the speculative-realist sensibility. But what Lovecraft gives us here is all that can be given. In other words, it is the very "weirdness" of this moment – that is, the dislocation between our experience and our ability to rationalize our experience – that prevents him from exploring further what is expressed in this uncanny moment. The only observation that Lovecraft can make is that something profoundly queer is happening in this moment. Apart from the impossible mental image that he crafts to express it, nothing else can be said of the moment in which "an angle which was acute [...] behaved as if it were obtuse."

Understood like this, such concentration on the weird in literature is hardly something upon which a new literary criticism can rest. Indeed, in addition to the end-limit that it imposes on readings, such a sustained insistence on the significance of the weird actually makes us look back towards a Romantic sense of things, "where if nature speaks at all it is only in languages that are unintelligible or threatening" (Altieri 2007, 83). The weird is undoubtedly an important issue for a literary criticism that respects the basic tenets of speculative realism, but it is not rich enough as an individual concept to sustain a program of criticism or, in fact, to intimate the nuanced demands of an object-oriented account of things.

So, although previous work on the relationship between or

intersection of object-oriented philosophy and literary criticism has certainly lit interesting avenues for further investigation, none, to my mind at least, has offered a strategy by which one can claim to "do" a literary criticism that is informed by speculative-realist thought. This then is what I want to concern myself with for the remaining section of this chapter. What might a speculative-realist literary criticism look like? What should the object-oriented literary critic "do" with literature?

Let us begin by recalling what we might think of as the most significant assertions that I have made in the previous chapters. First is the assertion that the literary text that we hold in our hand is a machine. That is to say, literary texts operate on inputs in order to produce outputs just like any other object in the world. Importantly though, if the literary text is a machine then it is an incorporeal machine. This observation means a good many things, but for us the important idea to take away is that in order for the literary text to act in the world it needs to couple with a reader. Without a reader, every literary machine is dormant – at best, a site of potential. Once coupled with a reader, who we must also think of as a machine (for precisely the same reasons of thinking of the literary text as a machine), a new machine forms – a reading machine. This reading machine effectively marks the new "powers" of the reader (and the text for that matter). That is to say, the encounter between text and reader in the new assemblage of the reading machine changes the way in which the reader can act in the world. Such change happens as a result of the communion between text and reader through the mechanism of the imagination. The text fires the reader's imagination in an untold number of unanticipated ways, and it is this change to the imaginative landscape of the reader that has the potential to radically change the way in which the reader acts in the world.

If we think of the act of literature like this then it is clear that the literary critic can no longer be interested in a quest to reveal an objective meaning or logic that is supposed to belong to the text in hand. We have already argued this point. But, surprisingly, neither does it mean that we have to come down on the subjective side of things. Rather, to understand the act of literature as a function of a particular reading machine is to collapse the subject/object dialectic and in so doing orient all proper questions of literature towards a consideration of the specific effects that a particular reading machine produces – that is, to ask what machines *do*. In other words, one critiques literature not by "mining it" (either by undermining it or over-mining it, as Harman would say) but by considering the effect that it has on a particular reader. What then do I mean by "effect"? Well, here I am happy to follow the rather broad account of "effect" given across the writing of Gilles Deleuze and Félix Guattari – that is, effect understood as both the way in which the reading machine changes the ideas and feelings of its reader *and* the way in which those "changes in the reader's dispositions, attitudes and behaviors," as Bruce Baugh observes, "link up with other forces affecting the reader, particularly social and political forces" (2000, 34). As such, considering the effect of a reading machine is not only a question of detailing a changing way of thinking; it is also a question of detailing where such changes eventually lead the reader in her encounter with the world.

This means that the object-oriented literary critic is primarily interested in tracing the private products of a particular reading machine. As such, the questions that one poses of a text should not concern its supposed meaning but rather its functioning. One simply asks of a text, "does it work for me?" It is a simple question, and one that belies the dramatic shift in the art of literary criticism that it demands if one is to respond to it with any degree of good faith. By asking whether a novel or a poem "works for me," the reader draws attention to the fact that it is the reader herself who is responsible for constituting the meaning of a text and, more importantly, that the literary work is only to be understood and evaluated in terms of the reader's own goals and values. Here, any residual sense one may carry of a universal or transcendental meaning embedded in the text finally evaporates. All texts are to be judged on a private scale, designed by the reader herself, which calculates whether or not a text increases the power of the reader to act in the world (that is to say, the extent to which the text fires the reader's imagination and in so doing alters the reader's perception and action in the world).

Now, in just the same way that one can almost hear the gasp of the literary critic who hears Harman's notion of literary modification for the first time, one can almost hear the sigh of the critic who thinks that such a turn to the private evaluation of literature is just another moment of tiresome postmodern posturing. "Surely," they would say, "Chaucer, Shakespeare, and Dickens wrote great literature regardless of whether this or that person enjoys reading it." And our answer would be, "Perhaps." Certainly, a great many people have found much value in these writers, but it is also true that they have been responsible for distancing a great many people from reading as a whole. Because others find value in these literary works does not mean that all readers should find them valuable. Regardless of how one feels about a private evaluation of Shakespeare that might find his writing impenetrable, one must at least respect such appraisal as being honest – and as speaking only of how *one particular reader* fails to connect with the work of *one particular writer*. Of course, that same reader might find the work of Ben Johnson or Christopher Marlowe much more inspiring (although it is unlikely!). The point is that to ask whether a novel "works for me" is ultimately to take responsibility for one's own engagement with literature, something which is immediately lost when we choose to defer judgment by citing the work of others or employing the standard measures of contemporary literary criticism. For this reason alone, considering the products of a reading machine is a valuable act.

Once the literary critic turns away from the pursuit of uncovering a universal textual meaning in favor of one that concerns itself with the products of a particular reading machine like this, then a remarkable transformation of the landscape of literary studies occurs. If readings of literary works are profoundly private affairs, then those so-called important and influential secondary texts that accrue around literary works (and those inherited reading practices that direct the way in which we engage a text) must lose gravity and eventually give way to such readings. That is to say, those authoritative essays and books that have traditionally focused our reading of, say, Shakespeare cannot retain their position of influence in the realm of private reading. Private reading simply has no need or role for such writing.

However, that is not to say that this kind of private reading is a purely individual affair. As Fredric Jameson writes, all literature "comes before us as the always-already-read" (2002, ix). What he means by this is that it is nigh-on impossible to read a famous novel or poem, or look at a famous painting, drawing or sculpture, or listen to a famous piece of music or watch a famous play or film, without being conscious of the contexts in which the text had been reproduced, drawn upon, alluded to, or parodied. Take for example George Orwell's *Nineteen Eighty-Four* (1949). Orwell's novel is so often invoked in contemporary discussions of contemporary Western culture (as a warning against totalitarian thought or a warning against surveillance societies) that it feels as though we know the book even if we have never actually read it. As an aside, it is one of my own speculations that this vicarious knowledge of Orwell's novel explains the fact that it is the book that most UK readers knowingly lie about having read.[16] But what such vicarious knowledge of literature tells us (and we have this kind of knowledge of all literature to one degree or another, regardless of whether it is a "new" book or not) is that every reading machine is at birth a socially sensitive assemblage. That is to say, every reading machine is embedded in the swell of collective ideas that inform the attitudes of a particular culture – morality, ethics, politics, and gender being just some of the obvious collective positions through which we think. As such, it would be wrong to think of the private reading of a text as a solitary act.

Nonetheless, every private reading is an original or unique way of thinking through the possibilities of a particular literary text. If the contemporary literary critic gasped at the suggestion of literary modification and sighed at private evaluation as a means to measure texts, then claiming that every private reading is unique is likely to stop the same critic's heart! But on this matter, I really must insist. When we read a literary work, we do so as if for the first time regardless of whether it is our first encounter with the text or our tenth. I can say this with absolute certainty because of what we have learned about the essential characteristics of readers and texts – that is, readers are complex machinic assemblages that are constantly evolving, and texts are incorporeal packets of potential. Because these objects are not rigid and therefore stable machines, every encounter that they will have will give off different effects. In other words, every reading will be different to the last, and therefore "new."

Another way to think of this is by using the figure of the conversation. Even though the same two people may talk about the same issue day-after-day, one can be absolutely certain that they will never have the same conversation twice. The ideas expressed may be the same, some of the words and phrases of previous conversations may be repeated from time-to-time, certain points of contention or observation may reappear, but the conversation itself will never be identical to a previous conversation. This is because time and experience impacts on us all and changes us both biologically and intellectually. As such, what we think of as "those same two people" who talked about the same issue day-after-day are not, after all, the "same people." And it is this that is true of the formation of a reading machine – the terms of the encounter (the particular reader and the particular text) are never, ultimately, the same. Therefore, no two reading machines can ever (absolutely cannot!) produce the same effects (even if the two reading machines are formed by the coming together of the same reader and the same text). In short, every private reading is unique because it is the result of a unique encounter between reader and text.

So, what I am suggesting here is a literary criticism that turns away from the search for meaning in favor of one that simply traces the effects of private readings. The consequences of doing so, as I have briefly sketched above, are dramatic but ultimately liberatory for the reader. In this schema, literature is read by all and considered solely in terms of whether it resonates in one way or another with its individual reader (rather than its "readership"). Because of this, the notion of an authoritative reading or a privileged reading slips away to be replaced by the reader's own encounter with a text. And in this moment of the slip, what we witness is the radical democratization of literature – the moment in which literature is no longer a province dominated by the university professor or the professional literary critic. Literature is either that which "works for me" (to the extent that it increases my power to act in the world in some way or other) or it is something that does not. Yet, somewhat regardless of whether the encounter is productive or not, liter-ature shows itself to be not some rarefied form of expression that exists other to this world in which we live (as some would have it),[17] but rather something that is part and parcel of the very fabric of the world.

How then to talk of this style of literary criticism that abandons the act of retrieval or mining for one of personal invention and creation? Well, I think our key term here is "exper-imental." What this private criticism of effects gestures towards is an experimental form of reading. In order to understand what this means, it is worth reminding ourselves of the etymology of the term "experiment." Experiment comes into the English language through the Latin *experiri*, which means "to try." The first dimension of our experimental form of reading is then marked by the impulse to try – that is, to try things out, to improvise, to create, to invent (responses to situations). But interestingly, *experiri* is also the root of the English word "experience." And it is this that gives us the second dimension to our experimental form of reading. Of course, "experience" means to observe, to encounter, but, importantly, it also means to consider. Stressed in this way, towards the act of contemplation, our style of criticism cannot be satisfied with making simple observations on or about the effects of a reading machine. Rather, it is incumbent on us to reflect on our creations and inventions and in so doing make something of them. In this way, our experimental form of reading is concerned first and foremost with pragmatics – that is, relating our speculations on the world to the fact of acting within it. And for this reason, its quarry is always "what's coming into being, what's new, what's taking shape" (Deleuze 1995, 106) in the formation of the reading machine.

In this sense then, our conversation with literature – that is, the formation of the reading machine – is one that is inevitably directed towards the act of creation or invention. To read, as Deleuze says, is to read "as a series of experiments for each reader" (1995, 9). Of course, this does not mean that one throws away our rational brain in pursuit of the infinitely outrageous (although we could, if that was the ground of our experiment). As we have already noted, Alfred North Whitehead has made clear enough the fact that considered speculation plays an intimate role in the progression of scientific thought. Nor does it mean that we can only hope to discover "that the same work means different things to different people, or that it has a meaning that is ambiguous or undecidable" (Baugh 2000, 37). How tiresome would this "conclusion" quickly grow to be once we had read it for the second or third time? What it does mean is that we encounter a text without anticipating what the result of that encounter might be. In the true sense of experiment, our experimental form of reading is not in place in order to prove or disprove whatever thesis we might bring to the text. Remember: experiment means among other things to try things out, to improvise, and to create. Rather, our experimental reading aims simply to detail why and where a text eventually leads us; it compels us to answer the question of what new concepts and ideas have evolved from the formation of a particular reading machine (if any).

For this reason, and it is a point worth emphasizing, if this radical new reading strategy resists anything at all it is the impulse to try and determine *how* a reading machine works. Speculative realism tells us that this kind of question can have no other result than the erosion of the object of enquiry (the text in hand). Such attempts to understand the mechanics of the reading machine can only lead us back towards the standard forms of literary interpretation – that is, analysis of character, plot, theme, symbol, and so on – and in so doing risk an untimely rediscovery of the practice of New Criticism. Again, the reading machine understood as a machinic assemblage necessarily resists any such effort to gain mastery over its functioning, for such mining can only hope to elucidate the character of the machines that are constitutive of the larger assemblage. When it is the effects of the reading machine itself that the literary critic is interested in tracing, such "knowledge" of the constitutive machines is ultimately worthless – what would one know of water if we only had knowledge of the individual elements of hydrogen and oxygen?

Thinking of literary criticism as experimentation in this way does away with interpretation and heads the critic towards something like a "creative criticism" – a style of literary criticism that I would say is defined by a genuine recognition of the creative moments by which the reader becomes writer in the act of critique. For sure, creative criticism has been around for a long time – it has certainly gone by many names: post-criticism, deformative criticism, anarcho-scholasticism, ficto-criticism, visionary criticism, Other criticism, and philosophic criticism, to name just a few[18] – but regardless of the guises it has adopted over the years, as Stephen Benson and Clare Connors make clear in the introduction to their recent edited anthology on the subject, creative criticism has always been "concerned with its own form and with its own writerliness" (2014, 26). For this reason, one could argue that creative criticism has always been a more honest form of criticism than those other forms pursued in the twentieth century. In its commitment to restore "the passion and lostness and wonderment of reading" (Benson and Connors 2014, 2), it absolves itself to act in a way that appeals to the scientific mind – that is to say, it does away with the pretense of objectivity that other forms of criticism have claimed for themselves to one degree or another over the years. And it is in this abandonment that we should recognize the honesty of creative criticism, for every form of literary criticism has always been an exercise in personal creativity. That is to say, literary criticism has always been about personal engagement and inventiveness; it is just that it has looked to sublimate this private aspect of reading in the hope of talking to the universal or the transcendental. Who, though, can read Derrida or Deleuze or Michel Serres without noting the innovative use of language that colors their work (let alone the innovation of thought that powers it)?

To my mind at least, the way in which creative criticism acknowledges and embraces a creative, innovative, inventive, and experimental private reading marks a return of the essay genre to its roots, which is to say to the writing of the sixteenth-century French thinker, Michel de Montaigne. Montaigne's essays were wayward affairs – personal, anti-dogmatic, and idiosyncratic pieces that revealed the tentative and exploratory nature of his intellectual engagement with the world.[19] But that is not to say that they were things of whimsy, for Montaigne's essays captured both senses of the way in which the word is employed in French – *essai* means both "to try / to attempt" and "trial / test." As Benson and Connors note, this means that for Montaigne "the word had a bolder sense [...] than that of an abashed attempt; a sense to do with toughening it out or running a gauntlet, seeing how far you can go, like a test-your-strength machine at the fairground" (2014, 7). It is this steel of purpose demanded by taking on a truly exploratory task that much contemporary scholarship lacks and upon which the very best creative criticism rests. If such criticism leads to the essay form, then it must be an essay freed of convention. To do justice to the idea or the concept being explored or invented by the critic, the essay genre as it is practiced today must give way if necessary. The point is to allow criticism the opportunity to open up or open out to texts in whichever way it is thought best to explore a particular idea. In short, it is to make every kind of reading possible, even if that reading is expressed in other ways to the word on the page (for example, *Radiohead*'s "2+2=5" understood as a musical essay on Orwell's *Nineteen Eighty-Four*, or Millais's *Ophelia* understood as a visual essay on Shakespeare's *Hamlet*).

Understood like this, the aim of experimental reading or creative criticism is to make real Michel Foucault's dream of a better species of criticism. In a famous interview in which the infamous French philosopher questions the very idea of the contemporary philosopher, Foucault says of the art of criticism (literary or otherwise):

I can't help but dream about a kind of criticism that would try not to judge but to bring [...] an idea to life; it would light fires, watch the grass grow, listen to the wind, and catch the sea foam in the breeze and scatter it. It would multiply not judgments but signs of existence; it would summon them, drag them from their sleep. Perhaps it would invent them sometimes – all the better. All the better. (qtd. in Rabinow 1997, 323)

In this short passage, Foucault maps out perfectly the markers of the kind of experimental-reading practice that I have been gesturing towards in this chapter – the death of judgment as a universal or transcendental schema, the proliferation of passion and private engagement, and the celebration of imagination and invention. The result, as I see it, is not only a democratization of literature but also a grand egalitarian view of our response to it.

We have reached a point, then, where I think we can now put down the bones of what a reading practice that responds to the concerns of speculative realism might look like:

1. The space-clearing gesture

Reject the very idea of a privileged reading. You are the most important reader of the book in your hand. The ideas of others might help you to think in interesting new ways about the books you read, but such readings should never occupy more than a second thought. Your reading, being conscious of your response to the literary text, is that to which your emotional and intellectual energy should be devoted.

2. Begin

Do not be seduced by what is our trained impulse to interpret a text. Many of us have been taught how to read, which is to say how to begin to interpret or make sense of a literary work. But let us say for one last time that even if we could claim to know the meaning of a text, doing so would not help us to understand the effects of our reading machine. Interpretation is a process of identification – a game of substitution that we learn to play: *this means that (but not this other)*. Because it works in this way, when we interpret a text what we are actually doing is flattening it out

– "Oh, I get it! The book is about..." But let us listen to Deleuze and Guattari on this point:

> A book has neither object nor subject; it is made of variously formed matters, and very different dates and speeds. To attribute the book to a subject is to overlook this working of matters [...] In a book, as in all things, there are lines of articulation or segmentarity, strata and territories; but also lines of flight, movements of deterritorialization and destratification. Comparative rates of flow on these lines produce phenomena of relative slowness and viscosity, or, on the contrary, of acceleration and rupture. All this, lines and measurable speeds, constitutes an assemblage. A book is an assemblage of this kind, and as such is unattributable. (1999, 4)

This conceptually demanding description of a book is full of the kind of exotic language that characterizes the work of Deleuze and Guattari, but the point they make here is, I think, perfectly clear – a text is never "about" anything, and to read it as though it is has the effect of smoothing out the very contours of the language that gives the specific literary work its character and renders it unique. For sure, a book may affect us in some way, but it is far more likely that it will be a particular passage from a book, a particular phrase even, that will continue to resonate with us long after the book has been returned to the bookshelf. "The devil," as somebody once said, "is in the detail," and so it is here, for it is the detail – that is, the text *as it is* and not as we interpret it to be – with which we engage and that fires our imagination.

3. Begin again

Experiment with the text! You will surely conduct your own experiments, so take the following as mere suggestion of how one might begin to experiment with literary texts. First, own the text (see point 1). Then, bring literary texts into conversation across time and space. Embrace a utopian sense of things – that texts belong to "no-place" despite being written by a person inhabiting one tiny piece of the world (and therefore accept the conclusion that there is no such thing as "national literature"). Intentionally read anachronistically, for the literary work is unaware of when it was written. Besides, we have been reading things out of chronological order all our lives. Perhaps you should dwell on the unfamiliar – the weird, the uncanny, moments of disidentification and defamiliarization – but never in order to try and domesticate it (which is to say, to bring it into a knowledge system). Rather, let us see where it leads the reading machine and to what it encourages it to connect.

4. Persist

Have the courage of Montaigne to trace and detail all of the effects released by your reading machine. Sometimes this will lead you to painful places; other times to places of great joy. But it will always lead you to unanticipated, unknown places if you allow it. It is from here, this space of the nameless, that the very best creative criticism will emerge.

5. Create and innovate

Read as a Deleuzian philosopher and in so doing look to produce new concepts by which to know the world. In other words, speculate and create.

Hopefully, it will be clear that this is a reading practice that is ultimately geared towards increasing the reader's power to act. And this point alone should make plain that the experimental reading and creative criticism that I outline above is no easy ride for the literary critic. Indeed, the kind of self-awareness called for by this reading practice and the stress it places on creativity and innovation demand more from the reader than most are willing to give.

7

A Few Concluding Remarks

Thinking, analyzing, inventing [...] are not anomalous acts; they are the normal respiration of the intelligence. To glorify the occasional performance of that function, to hoard ancient and alien thoughts, to recall with incredulous stupor what the *doctor universalis* thought, is to confess our laziness or our barbarity. Every man should be capable of all ideas, and I understand that in the future this will be the case.
– Pierre Menard (Borges 2000, 70)

Jorge Luis Borges certainly had a way with words, and those he placed into the mouth of Pierre Menard here speak directly to the project at hand. Indeed, my conclusion to the question of what an object-oriented inflected literary criticism might look like is found in Menard's vision of a utopian future for criticism. The practice of experimental reading captured through a radical criticism that is dedicated to the creation of new concepts is an attempt to raise the critic from his lethargy (if not barbarity). It opens up the idea of literature so that it can be engaged in an almost limitless number of ways – it encourages everyone to have an idea about the book in their hand and to have confidence that their idea is valuable (at least to themselves – actually, only to themselves).

But it is important to emphasize that object-oriented literary criticism does all of this not through some esoteric framework that only some of the very best scholars around the world can follow; it does so by appealing to what Menard calls here "the normal respiration of the intelligence." And I think it is this that marks the great finding of this book. *Object-oriented philosophy gives birth to a profoundly egalitarian style of literary criticism that is premised on a grand democratization of Literature proper.* At no point does object-oriented literary criticism, as I have written it here, require anything more of the reader than an ability to pay attention to her own responses to the text in her hand – to note how the text changes (or reinforces) her perception and account of things. It does not require you to have an understanding of semiotics, or the formal elements of a text, or a sense of literary history. It simply requires you to read, and in the act of reading remain mindful of your reaction (emotional, ethical, political, and so on) to the text. This is how we have always read, but it has taken an examination of the intersection between speculative realism and literature to rediscover it.

So, an object-oriented literary criticism takes us back to embracing the products of an honest intellectual engagement with literature. For some, this will mark the death of the literary critic in the same way that Roland Barthes's observations on the polyvocal and intertextual composition of the literary text brought about the death of the author. However, it might be too soon to write that particular obituary. Over the hundred or so years that literary criticism has been a recognized industry, it has made undeniable progress – for example, it has given us both robust and intimate portraits of the figure of the author, the site of the text, and the importance of the reader. It has also identified foundational issues of which every new way of reading must be mindful – semiotics, representation, context, ideology, and power dynamics. Such work is simply too important to bury with a (prematurely) expired literary critic.

In light of this, I want to make clear here that the style of criticism that we have arrived at in this book is not one that looks to supplant other kinds of criticism. Rather, it is one that wants to run alongside them. Some criticism works because it explores the constitutive features of the text in hand (it is interested in thinking about those machines that make up the larger assemblage of the literary work). Other criticism works because it explores the (endless) relationships within which a literary work takes place. Object-oriented literary criticism works because it genuinely thinks of the text as an object in itself. That is to say, what I have been discussing on the pages of this book is not an approach to literature that claims to be somehow "better" than anything that has come before it, but rather another class of approach – a third style of criticism; one that maintains a sense of the literary text as an object in itself. The literary critic who chooses to engage the literary text in this way certainly looks different to the critics who have come before her (in the sense that they have very different concerns and think of the text in very different ways), but I do not think we can say quite yet that she has lived her last day!

In the introduction to this book, I wrote that the test of any new literary theory or style of criticism is what it empowers the critic to see or do that has not already been seen or done. I feel confident that the object-oriented literary criticism that I have outlined over the course of this book does indeed empower the critic to see and do "new" things with literature. Actually, that is not quite right – the object-oriented literary criticism that I write here is ultimately about recovering a forgotten way of reading, an honest way of reading that is schooled out of us early in our lives. Do I like this novel? Am I affected by this poem? What do I connect with or identify with in this short story? These are the essential questions of our encounter with literature that we need to relearn how to ask ourselves. For that, they are the essential questions by which our creative criticism will look to make sense of a world of failing machines.

Notes

1. That being said, I do not want to imply that the writing of Grant, Brassier, and Harman is in any way a reaction to the work of Meillassoux. Clearly, these writers were charting their own particular philosophical waters before Meillassoux introduced the notion of correlationism as a way to read the wider concerns of modern philosophy. That is to say, it is perhaps a matter of historical happenstance that these writers were ultimately concerned, in their own ways, with the relationship between mind and a mind-independent world of things.

2. Quotation modified. The original passage reads, "Wouldn't a truly mind-independent world make any representation of it, in thought or language, unreliable, if not impossible? On what grounds can we trust our theories if they could all be radically mistaken?" See Khlentzos (2001).

3. On the holographic universe, see Chown (2009). On the simulation hypothesis, see Bostrom (2003). And on the many-worlds interpretation, see Vilenkin (2007).

4. There are three significant editions of Baudelaire's *Fleurs du Mal* – the 1857, 1861, and 1868 editions. The 1861 edition is the result of a successful obscenity trial brought against the 1857 book by the French government. Six poems from the 1857 edition were removed from the 1861 edition, but thirty-two new poems were added in their place – including "Paysage." The 1868 edition was published a year after Baudelaire's death, and is the edition most studied today.

5. Quotation modified. Nicholls is talking here about Baudelaire's poem "Correspondances." The exact quotation reads, "Already 'Correspondences' predicts the psychological (or interior) landscape of the Symbolists, the natural setting of the poem no longer an ordinary, external one, but

rather a zone of the mind where objects pulse with the same inner vibration." See Nicholls (1995, 26).

6. Let us leave aside for the moment the rather awkward observation that in Genesis 10 the sons of Noah and their offspring had already been "divided in their lands; every one after his tongue, after their families, in their nations" (10: 5, 10: 20, 10: 31).

7. It is unclear in which language God spoke to Adam (2: 16–17), but conventional scholarship has it that it was a language of interior illumination. The first words from a human mouth are those uttered by Adam upon seeing Eve for the first time: "And Adam said, This is now bone of my bones, and flesh of my flesh: she shall be called Woman, because she was taken out of Man" (2: 23).

8. See Grusin (2015).

9. Of course, the consequence of this reading of encounters is that every single object in the world is understandable in terms of the encounters it can have with every other object of the universe. It is more proof then that an attempt to understand the essential character of a particular object is a fool's errand. How to understand the way in which the wind or a bee encounters a hat, let alone a milliner? Perhaps the best way to think of this argument is as the next step to Thomas Nagel's rightly famous essay, "What is it like to be a bat?" See Nagel (1974).

10. See Dawkins (2010). Chapter 11 is dedicated to the way in which biological bodies exhibit their ancient past in both obvious and unexpected ways.

11. Still, Brooks was not quite willing to concede the significance of such an observation. After making the initial point he quickly tempers it with: "Yet, to put meaning and valuation of a literary work at the mercy of any and every individual would reduce the study of literature to reader psychology and to the history of taste." See Brooks (1995, 87).

12. *Il miglior fabbro* comes from line 117 of Canto XXVI of Dante's "Purgatorio," the second cantica of *The Divine Comedy*. Here Dante describes the troubadour Arnaut Daniel as "the best craftsman of the mother tongue."

13. For merely one example of the scientific evidence to which I refer, see Berns *et al* (2013).

14. See Shubin (2009).

15. I refer of course to Marcel Duchamp's *L.H.O.O.Q.* (1919).

16. See Brown (2009).

17. See for example the work of Pascale Casanova, who has described world literature as "a literary universe relatively independent of the everyday world and its political divisions, whose boundaries and operational laws are not reducible to those of everyday political space." See Casanova (2004, xii).

18. I borrow this list of previous incarnations of what is today called creative criticism from Benson and Connors. See Benson and Connors (2014, 2).

19. I borrow this description of Montaigne's essays from Benson and Connors (2014).

Works Cited

Altieri, Charles (2007), "The Sensuous Dimension of Literary Experience: An Alternative to Materialist Theory," *New Literary History* 38 (1), 71–98.

Attridge, Derek (2004), *J.M. Coetzee and the Ethics of Reading*. Chicago: University of Chicago Press.

Ballard, J.G. (1996), *A User's Guide to the Millennium*. London: HarperCollins.

Barthes, Roland (1977), *Image-Music-Text*, translated by Stephen Heath. London: Fontana.

Bassnett, Susan (1994), *Translation Studies*. London: Routledge.

Baudelaire, Charles (1995), *Baudelaire: Selected Writings on Art and Literature*, edited and translated by P. E. Charvet. London: Penguin.

Baugh, Bruce (2000), "How Deleuze can help us make literature work," in *Deleuze and Literature*, edited by Ian Buchanan and John Marks, 34–56. Edinburgh: Edinburgh University Press.

Benson, Stephen and Clare Connors, eds. (2014), *Creative Criticism: An Anthology and Guide*. Edinburgh: Edinburgh University Press.

Berns, Gregory, Kristina Blaine, Michael Prietula, and Brandon Pye (2013), "Short- and Long-Term Effects of a Novel on Connectivity in the Brain," *Brain Connectivity* 3 (6), 590-600.

Borges, Jorge Luis (2000), *Labyrinths: Selected Stories and Other Writings*, edited by Donald Yates and James Irby. London: Penguin.

Bostrom, Nick (2003), "Are You Living In a Computer Simulation?" *Philosophical Quarterly* 53 (211), 243–255.

Brassier, Ray (2007), *Nihil Unbound: Enlightenment and Extinction*. London: Palgrave Macmillan.

Braver, Lee (2013), "On Not Settling the Issue of Realism," *Speculations: A Journal of Speculative Realism* (4), 11–14.

Brooks, Cleanth (1947), *The Well-Wrought Urn: Studies in the Structure of Poetry.* New York: Harcourt, Brace & World.

—- (1995), *Community, Religion, and Literature: Essays by Cleanth Brooks.* Columbia: University of Missouri Press.

Brown, Mark (2009), "Our guilty secrets: the books we only say we've read," *The Guardian: Books.* http://www.theguardian.com/books/2009/mar/05/uk-reading-habits-1984

Bryant, Levi (2014), *Onto-Cartography: An Ontology of Machines and Media.* Edinburgh: Edinburgh University Press.

Bryant, Levi, Nick Srnicek and Graham Harman, eds. (2011), *The Speculative Turn: Continental Materialism and Realism.* Melbourne: Re.press.

Casanova, Pascale (2004), *The World Republic of Letters,* translated by M.B. DeBevoise. Cambridge, MA: Harvard University Press.

Chown, Marcus (2009), "Our world may be a giant hologram," *New Scientist.* https://www.newscientist.com/article/mg20126911-300-our-world-may-be-a-giant-hologram/

Culler, Jonathan (2004), *Structuralist Poetics: Structuralism, Linguistics and the Study of Literature.* London: Routledge.

Dawkins, Richard (2010), *The Greatest Show on Earth: The Evidence for Evolution.* London: Black Swan.

Deleuze, Gilles (1995), *Negotiations,* translated by Martin Joughin. New York: Columbia University Press.

Deleuze, Gilles and Félix Guattari (1994), *What is Philosophy?* translated by Graham Burchell and Hugh Tomlinson. London: Verso.

—- (1999), *A Thousand Plateaus: Capitalism and Schizophrenia 2,* translated by Brian Massumi. London: Athlone.

Derrida, Jacques (1978), "Structure, Sign and Play in the Discourse of the Human Sciences" in *Writing and Difference.* London: Routledge.

Eco, Umberto (1998), *Serendipities: Language and Lunacy*, translated by William Weaver. London: Weidenfeld & Nicolson.

—- (2003), *Mouse or Rat? Translation as Negotiation*. London: Weidenfeld & Nicolson.

Ghil, René (1886), *Traité du verbe*. Paris: Giraud.

Grant, Iain Hamilton (2011), "Mining Conditions: A Response to Harman" in *The Speculative Turn: Continental Materialism and Realism*, edited by Levi Bryant, Nick Srnicek and Graham Harman, 41–46. Melbourne: Re.press.

Gratton, Peter (2014), *Speculative Realism: Problems and Prospects*. London: Bloomsbury.

Grusin, Richard, ed. (2015), *The Nonhuman Turn*. Minneapolis: University of Minnesota Press.

Harman, Graham (2011a), *The Quadruple Object*. Winchester: Zero Books.

—- (2011b), "The Road to Objects," *Continent* 1 (3), 171–179.

—- (2012), "The Well-Wrought Broken Hammer: Object-Oriented Literary Criticism," *New Literary History* 43 (2), 183–203.

—- (2013), *Bells and Whistles: More Speculative Realism*. Winchester: Zero Books.Iser, Wolfgang (1972), "The Reading Process: A Phenomenological Approach," *New Literary History* 3 (2), 279–299.

Jameson, Fredric (2002), *The Political Unconscious: Narrative as a Socially Symbolic Act*. London: Routledge.

Joy, Eileen (2013), "Weird Reading," *Speculations: A Journal of Speculative Realism* (4), 28–34.

Khlentzos, Drew (2001), "Challenges to Metaphysical Realism," *Stanford Encyclopedia of Philosophy*. http://plato.stanford.edu/entries/realism-sem-challenge/

Krafft-Ebing, Richard Von (1939), *Psychopathia Sexualis: A Medico-Forensic Study*, with introduction and supplement by Victor Robinson. London: Heinemann.

Kramer, Peter and Paola Bressan (2015), "Humans as Superorganisms: How Microbes, Viruses, Imprinted Genes, and Other Selfish Entities Shape Our Behavior," *Perspectives on Psychological Science* 10 (4), 464–481.

Kristeva, Julia (1986), "Word, Dialogue and Novel," in *The Kristeva Reader*, edited by Toril Moi and translated by Alice Jardine et al, 34–61. New York: Columbia University Press.

Kwasny, Melissa, ed. (2004), *Toward the Open Field: Poets on the Art of Poetry 1800–1950*. Connecticut: Wesleyan University Press.

Lloyd, Rosemary, ed. and trans. (1988), *Selected Letters of Stéphane Mallarmé*. Chicago: University of Chicago Press.

Lovecraft, H.P. (1999), *The Call of Cthulhu and Other Weird Stories*, edited by S.T. Joshi. London: Penguin.

Meillassoux, Quentin (2009), *After Finitude: An Essay on the Necessity of Contingency*, translated by Ray Brassier. London: Continuum.

Moran, Richard (1994), "The Expression of Feeling in Imagination," *The Philosophical Review* 103 (1), 75–106.

Morton, Timothy (2012), "An Object-Oriented Defense of Poetry," *New Literary History* 43 (2), 205–224.

Nagel, Thomas (1974), "What is it like to be a bat?" *The Philosophical Review* 83 (4), 435–450.

Nicholls, Peter (1995), *Modernisms*. London: Macmillan.

Propp, Vladimir (1958), *Morphology of the Folktale*, translated by Laurence Scott. Austin: University of Texas Press.

Rabinow, Paul, ed. (1997), *Ethics, Subjectivity and Truth: The Essential Works of Michel Foucault 1954–1984*. New York: The New Press.

Selden, Raman, Peter Widdowson and Peter Brooker (2005), *A Reader's Guide to Contemporary Literary Theory*. London: Pearson.

Shklovsky, Viktor (1965), "Art as Technique" in *Russian Formalist Criticism: Four Essays*, edited and translated by Lee T. Lemon and Marion J. Reis, 3–24. Lincoln: University of Nebraska Press.

Shubin, Neil (2009), *Your Inner Fish: The Amazing Discovery of Our*

375-Million-Year-Old Ancestor. London: Penguin.

Sleator, Roy D. (2010), "The Human Superorganism: Of Microbes and Men," *Medical Hypotheses* 74 (2), 214–215.

Travers, Martin, ed. (2001), *European Literature from Romanticism to Postmodernism: A Reader in Aesthetic Practice*. London: Continuum.

Tyson, Lois (2006), *Critical Theory Today: A User-Friendly Guide*. London: Routledge.

Verene, Donald Phillip (2009), *Speculative Philosophy*. New York: Lexington Books.

Vilenkin, Alex (2007), *Many Worlds in One: The Search for Other Universes*. New York: Hill and Wang.

Weller, Sam (2010), "Ray Bradbury, The Art of Fiction No. 203," *Paris Review* 192 (Spring).

Whitehead, Alfred North (1985), *Process and Reality: Corrected Edition*, edited by David Ray Griffin and Donald W. Sherburne. New York: The Free Press.

Wimsatt, W. K. Jr. and M. C. Beardsley (1946), "The Intentional Fallacy," *The Sewanee Review* 54 (3), 468–488.

Contemporary culture has eliminated both the concept of the public and the figure of the intellectual. Former public spaces – both physical and cultural – are now either derelict or colonized by advertising. A cretinous anti-intellectualism presides, cheerled by expensively educated hacks in the pay of multinational corporations who reassure their bored readers that there is no need to rouse themselves from their interpassive stupor. The informal censorship internalized and propagated by the cultural workers of late capitalism generates a banal conformity that the propaganda chiefs of Stalinism could only ever have dreamt of imposing. Zer0 Books knows that another kind of discourse – intellectual without being academic, popular without being populist – is not only possible: it is already flourishing, in the regions beyond the striplit malls of so-called mass media and the neurotically bureaucratic halls of the academy. Zer0 is committed to the idea of publishing as a making public of the intellectual. It is convinced that in the unthinking, blandly consensual culture in which we live, critical and engaged theoretical reflection is more important than ever before.